THE GUN GRABBERS

Alan Gottlieb

MERRIL PRESS

BELLEVUE WASHINGTON

Acknowledgements

I wish to express my deepest gratitude to the Executive Director of the Second Amendment Foundation, Michael Kenyon, who worked closely with me on this project; to Gun Week Executive Editor Joseph Tartaro who provided not only a wealth of contemporary historical knowledge but also profound insight into the workings of the Gun Grabber mentality; to Gun Week contributing editor Ron Arnold for researching source materials, fact checking and editing the manuscript; and to John M. Snyder, Washington lobbyist of the Citizens Committee for the Right to Keep and Bear Arms who shared his tremendous grasp of the legislative process for Chapter Five and who also dug out the contribution list of Handgun Control, Inc. Political Action Committee from the labyrinth of Federal Elections Commission data files. Of course, this book would never have been written if it were not for the hundreds of thousands of individuals who have contributed to the Second Amendment Foundation's outstanding programs and projects.

Copies of this book may be purchased from the publishers for $14.95. All inquiries and catalog requests should be addressed to Merril Press, P.O. Box 1682, Bellevue, Washington 98009. Telephone 206-455-7009.

Library of Congress Cataloging in Publication data
Gottlieb, Alan M.
    The gun grabbers.

    Includes index

    1. Gun control — United States.   2. Gun control — United States — societies, etc.   3. Firearms — Law and legislation — United States.   I. Title.
HV7436.G68   1986   363.3'3'0973   86-869

ISBN: 0-936783-00-1

Contents

Dedication:
To
Julie, Amy Jean and Sarah Merril
my
wife and children
And
to the thousands of good people who
believe in me enough to encourage me
with their prayers and support—even
though we may never have a chance to meet
face to face.

Introduction
by Senator Steve Symms

Gun owners today could have no better book in their hands than this one. It's fast-paced. It's readable. But most importantly, it is a hard-hitting expose of those who would act to limit Americans' right to keep and bear arms. These gun grabbers, as author Alan M. Gottlieb dubs them, have organized a well-funded network of anti-gun activists. The sophistication of the gun-control coalition may come as a surprise—and a warning—to gun-owning Americans.

Gun owners know well how right Thomas Jefferson was when he wrote, "Eternal vigilance is the price of liberty." Gun owners know they must continually fight to preserve their rights in the face of anti-gun activists. And in order to do that effectively, as another famous saying goes, you have to "Know your enemy." But regrettably, up to now there has been no serious discussion of the anti-gun coalition's inner workings in the media. In *The Gun Grabbers*, Alan Gottlieb fills this void admirably with facts and figures and style.

I heartily recommend this book to you for several reasons. My own belief in the rights of gun owners is a good place to start. My position on gun control should be well enough known that I do not have to repeat it here, but let me state for the record that among other positive actions taken, I sponsored a bill called the Firearms Owners Rights Act to prohibit federal law enforcement and criminal justice funds from being given to cities and towns that prevent their residents from owning firearms. *The Gun Grabbers* takes a rational pro-gun stand that every gun owner can support.

Another reason I commend this book to you is the author. I've known Alan Gottlieb for years as the founder of the Second Amendment Foundation and president of the Citizens Committee for the Right to Keep and Bear Arms. He has stood at the forefront of most political battles over guns for nearly a decade. He's a fighter. He has the battle scars to prove it. He knows what he's talking about.

And, finally, you should read this book because, despite its serious subject, it's fun. You'll find its insights penetrating and its wit and humor refreshing. *The Gun Grabbers* may make your blood boil—whether you're pro-gun or anti-gun—but it will also make you think and smile and even laugh out loud.

What will come of it? You can rest assured that because Alan Gottlieb fearlessly names names and details the evidence in this book, many anti-gunners will want his hide nailed to the side of the barn. I doubt that anti-gun anger will frighten him much. Alan Gottlieb is no stranger to controversy. During the years I've known him, he has overcome one adversity after another. I'm well aware of his classic battle with the Internal Revenue Service. I've seen him go through meat-grinder situations and come out stronger than ever. The pro-gun movement has a truly remarkable advocate in Alan Gottlieb. It has a truly remarkable guide to the opposition in *The Gun Grabbers*.

1

The Gun Grabber Elite: Handgun Control, Inc.

"WHO REALLY RUNS CONGRESS, THE PEOPLE OR THE NRA? . . . NOW'S YOUR CHANCE TO TELL THE NRA TO GO TO HELL!" This is what the media love about Handgun Control, Inc., or HCI, as it is commonly known—its reasonableness, its temperance, its asininity.

For all its crass rhetoric and thoughtless bloody shirt-waving, HCI is indisputably the premier Gun Grabber group in America. It has the most members and the tightest organization—and potentially poses the greatest threat to gun owners. Every pro-gun citizen in the country needs to know something about this group, if for no other reason than to heed the old maxim "Know the enemy." Reading history can be dull, but you're more likely to find your blood boiling as we unfold the distasteful story of this organization. You'll see the way the opposition thinks and operates. You'll find out how much they count on blind luck for their issues and then relentlessly manipulate the facts, the media and the situation. You'll see that HCI's position on "gun control" has radicalized over the past decade. In its early years, HCI claimed that it merely wanted to "control" who had access to a handgun, but today, its leaders acknowledge that they want to ban all handguns.

Here, then, is a year-by-year account of the fascinating and vengeful Gun Grabber organization, Handgun Control, Inc.

YEAR 1: 1974

HCI started out originally as the National Council to Control Handguns (NCCH) in 1974, was known so until it changed its name in 1978. I know this is beginning to sound

1

like alphabet soup with all the abbreviations, but read on, you get used to it.

NCCH was incorporated in January 1974 as a 501(c)(4) nonprofit lobbying organization based in Washington, D.C., but even that was not the true beginning of the outfit. Back in the early 1970s, one Mark Borinsky, who had been robbed at gunpoint, founded the forerunner of NCCH at the University of Chicago as a campus group. Following graduation, he travelled to Washington, D.C. to join a gun-control organization—but finding none in existence, he opened the NCCH.

Nelson "Pete" T. (for Turner) Shields III teamed up with NCCH in May 1975, after his 22-year-old son Nick had been murdered in April 1974 in San Francisco by a member of that city's "Zebra" gang. Nick Shields' handgun-armed assassin was a member of a black-supremacy militant group bent on righting the wrongs of the pre-1865 American slave trade by randomly killing whites as they walked along the streets of San Francisco. Police officially attribute at least 21 white deaths to the "Zebra" killers, but the number of "Zebra" victims may actually be as high as 150 according to the book *Rage*.

After concluding that more controls were needed on the sale, transfer and possession of handguns, Shields took an unpaid leave of absence from his $40,000-a-year job as marketing manager of E. I. duPont in Wilmington, Delaware, and went to work in May 1975 as a volunteer lobbyist for NCCH. In late 1976, Shields took a formal early retirement from duPont.

YEAR 2: 1975

One of the activities of NCCH/HCI is to provide anti-gun testimony before congressional committees in an attempt to sway the congressmen to support new anti-gun legislation.

During one of its early testimonies, NCCH spokesmen revealed that they were not interested in just banning small handguns, but they were really interested in curtailing the individual possession of all handguns. In October 1975 the NCCH testified before a U.S. House Subcommittee on Crime hearings on firearm legislation. NCCH spokesmen at the hearing included Shields, James Campbell, NCCH co-ordinator of Legislative Task Force (and formerly general counsel of the National Commission on the Causes and Prevention of Violence), and Charles J. Orasin, NCCH's then assistant director. During the hearing, in response to a question concerning the viability of banning "Saturday Night Special" handguns, Campbell said, "Obviously the term "Saturday Night Special" is only an empty phrase unless there is something truly special about it so far as criminal use is concerned. But the most that can conceivably be claimed for the Special . . . is that in the past it may have been involved in as many as half of the handgun crimes being committed— but since half of the handguns being manufactured . . . fall within the definition of a Saturday Night Special, there is nothing significant in the statistic. The unique 'criminality' of the Saturday Night Special remains unproved."

From this statement it is readily apparent that NCCH makes no distinction between small "non sporting" handguns and large "sporting" handguns; they want to ban them all.

At that time the NCCH was circulating a position paper concerning the viability of whether handgun registration and gun owner licensing would curtail crime. Their position was:

"Such a bill would establish a large bureaucracy at considerable expense to the taxpayer. Mountains of paperwork and endless processing of forms would be required. It's doubtful that even the most efficient agency could keep up-to-date accurate records on every handgun, handgun owner and handgun transaction. We see the only truly effective handgun control legislation as that which would restrict handgun possession to a small number of appropriate groups: i.e. police, military, licensed security guards and licensed pistol clubs. . . . Our primary concern is whether a licensing and registration system would change the statistics of handgun violence. If a criminal used a handgun in a holdup, would it help to know it was stolen from John Smith, age 35, height 5'11; weight 170 lbs. If a husband kills his wife, would it change anything that there is a slip of paper in a drawer saying the pistol was registered."

According to a Council of Better Business Bureau report, NCCH's 1975 total income was $35,426 with expenses of

$49,050. The NCCH had three paid staff members and fifteen volunteers.

YEAR 3: 1976

By April 1976 NCCH was lobbying Congress for the enactment of H.R. 11193, which attempted to impose a 14-day waiting period for the police to undertake a criminal-history check on all handgun buyers; mandatory sentencing for use of a firearm in a federal crime of violence; a ban on the importation of parts for small handguns; and prohibit the purchase of more than one handgun in any 30-day period.

Despite NCCH's earlier criticisms of registration and licensing, Shields, who had become executive director earlier that year, gave an interview in the July 26, 1976 *New Yorker* magazine, saying:

"I'm convinced that we have to have federal legislation to build on. We're going to have to take one step at a time, and the first step is necessarily—given the political realities—going to be very modest. of course, it's true that politicians will then go home and say, 'This is a great law. The problem is solved. . . .' So then we'll have to start working again to strengthen that law, and then again to strengthen the next law, and maybe again and again. . . . Our ultimate goal— total control of handguns in the United States—is going to take time. My estimate is seven to ten years. The first problem is to slow down the increasing number of handguns being produced and sold in this country. The second problem is to get handguns registered. And the final problem is to make the possession of all handguns and all handgun ammunition— except for the military, policemen, licensed security guards, licensed sporting clubs, and licensed gun collectors—totally illegal."

Knowing for sure whether Pete Shields means what he says can be a problem. I recall a debate I had with him on a nationally syndicated television show originating in Detroit in May of 1976. Pete was throwing FBI firearms crime statistics around fast and loose, and I called him on it. "I think you're making up up those statistics," I said. The host—who was obviously sympathetic to the Gun Grabber cause—called for a commercial break in order to look up the real numbers. Off camera, the pertinent FBI report was examined. Sure enough, the firearms crime numbers Pete Shields had quoted were nowhere to be found. When we came back on camera, the host had to admit that Shields made up the statistics. As a result, Pete Shields has ever since refused to debate me.

During the year 1976 NCCH was very active in Massachusetts in supporting two anti-gun legislative proposals. First, NCCH helped to convince the state legislature to enact the controversial Bartley-Fox "Use a gun, go to jail" law. This law established a "mandatory" minimum one-year in jail sentence for anyone caught carrying a loaded gun without having a carrying-concealed- handgun permit, even if the individual was carrying for self-defense rather than planning to commit a crime.

The second project involved NCCH's support of a state-wide referendum measure (Question 5) which sought to ban individual ownership of handguns throughout Massachusetts. However, the measure was rejected 2-to-1 by the public at the November 2 general election.

Commenting on his defeat, Shields said, "We felt whether Question 5 won or failed, the absolute next step was to get basic federal legislation. Either way, we planned to spend the vast part of the next two years getting that—not a total ban, but a lesser level which would make state action possible." Looking towards the future, Shields commented: "We'll take any law we can get. We're prepared to win our battle in bits and pieces and we realize this is going to be a long, slow process."

Perhaps conveniently forgetting his earlier statements, Shields claimed in December that now he was opposed to a total handgun ban because, "We don't believe that even the most stringent handgun controls will end violent crime. The causes of crime in this country are too deeply rooted in such complicated problems as our criminal-justice system, delinquency, the lack of jobs, and all the social and economic inequities that our society hasn't been able to adjust to fairly."

Although Shields in September 1977 said "It's not long guns we're rallying against" and a 1976 Council of Better Business Bureau report claimed that "according to [NCCH] solicitation literature, the [NCCH] is not working for the control of rifles." The NCCH supported the enactment of Washington, D.C.'s "handgun freeze" ordinance in 1976, which had a hidden impact on long guns. This law prohibits anyone from obtaining and possessing a handgun that hadn't been registered with city police by February 1977, but it also requires that all rifles and shotguns had to be registered and stipulated that they had to be broken down and could not be kept loaded for self-defense. It is also illegal for city residents to possess ammunition which could not be chambered into the homeowner's registered firearms.

Although Shields contends that he is merely interested in banning "snubbies", his true belief can be drawn from his remarks in that July 26, 1976 *New Yorker* magazine article:

"The first problem is to slow down the increasing number of handguns being produce in this country. The second problem is to get handguns registered. And the final problem is to make the possession of all handguns and all handgun ammunition . . . totally illegal."

Due to higher visibility resulting from its two Massachusetts projects, NCCH's membership had risen to about 2,500 members by the close of 1976.

YEAR 4: 1977

In July, the NCCH requested the U.S. Bureau of Alcohol, Tobacco & Firearms (BATF) through its rule-making powers to require gunshops, dealers, manufacturers, importers and special collectors to report the theft of handguns to the BATF.

In its newsletter the NCCH said of its action: this "was the first time handgun control advocates have formally asked the Bureau to issue regulations dealing with handguns. . . . Assisting [NCCH attorney] Alan B. Sternstein were : James Cambell, Candace Kovacic, Jay Urwitz, Seth Davidson, Gregory Scott and Suzanne Ehrenburg. . . . The NCCH petition affords the Carter Administration an opportunity to address one important aspect of the handgun problem." However, sensing that the NCCH didn't have as much political clout as it claimed it did, the BATF didn't follow through on NCCH's request.

By its July 1977 *Washington Report* newsletter the NCCH

acknowledged its lackluster performance for several of its activities:

"The NCCH led an unsuccessful effort to have needed funds restored to the budget of the [BATF]. NCCH lobbied against the cut of two million dollars because it meant the elimination of some 100 positions. . . . Although unsuccessful, the NCCH through personal visits to some fifty members of the [House Appropriations] Committee came away with a better understanding of their positions on the handgun issue."

"NCCH is working closely with the Justice Department and Administration officials [Pres. Carter] as they draft the President's handgun control policy. The ongoing dialogue with Administration officials is unprecedented and reflects the serious desire of the President to address the handgun problem. NCCH is hopeful that the President will recommend comprehensive legislation in the coming weeks."

A *Parade* magazine article noted in its September 18, 1977 issue that the NCCH "already had helped bring about two dramatic victories [this year]." It was a major factor in a handgun control bill passed by the House Judiciary Committee in the last session of Congress—and it defeated the NRA in court in defending the constitutionality of handgun control legislation in the District of Columbia.

Shields even persuaded Sen. Ted Kennedy to write a fund-raising sales pitch letter for NCCH, in which the Hero of Chappaquidick said: "Your organizational efforts of a national constituency for handgun control will go far to help fill a void that has been a hindrance to positive legislative efforts."

By late 1977, NCCH was listing the following celebrities on its letterhead, some more celebrated than others:

Board of Directors:
Mrs. C. Minor Barringer, Chadds Ford, PA
Dr. Mark Borinsky, NCCH founder
Mrs. Nancy Butler, Founder of Georgians for Handgun
    Control
Mr. Robert DiGrazia, Police Chief of Montgomery
    County, MD

Hon. John Hechinger, Former chairman of District of
  Columbia City Council
Mrs. Lois W. Hess, Baltimore, MD
Mrs. Lillian Kaplan, Pres. of the Chicago Civic Disarmament
  Committee for Handgun Control
Mr. Maurice Rosenblatt, Washington, D.C.
Mr. Adolph Rosengarten, Wayne, PA
Mr. Carl Spitzer, Washington, D.C
Mr. Edward O. Welles, Washington, D.C.
Hon. Edmund G. Brown, Sr.
Mr. Lloyd N. Cutler
Dr. Milton Eisenhower
Dr. Russell W. Peterson

NCCH Sponsors:

Mr. Steve Allen
Mr. Arthur Ashe
Mrs. Marjorie Benton
Dr. Charles H. Browning
Sheriff John J. Buckley
Ms. Ellen Burstyn
Mr. Hal Holbrook
Mayor Maynard Jackson
Mr. Albert E. Jenner, Jr.
Ms. Ann Landers
Mr. Peter Lawford
Hon. Edward H. Levi
Ms. Margaret Mead
Dr. Karl Menninger
Rep. Abner Mikva
Mr. Patrick Murphy

Mr. George Newton, Jr.
Mr. Milton Rector
Mr. Will Rogers, Jr.
Hon. William Ruckleshaus
Rabbi Alexander M. Schindler
Mr. & Mrs. Neil Simon
Mr. Rod Steiger
Mr. Eli Wallach
Mr. James Whitmore
Mr. Stimson Bullitt
Ms. Nancy Ignatius
Mr. Neil Sullivan
Mr. Tige Andrews
Mr. Howard Duff
Mr. Mike Farrell
Mr. David Toma

Although one of President Carter's aides, Hamilton Jordan,
had said in a December 1976 *New Times* interview that "Carter will really go on gun control and really be tough. We're
going to get those bastards," Jimmy didn't deliver.

"The Carter Justice Department called in members of the
gun-control lobby to help draft a new federal handgun-control
law in August [1977]"—according to anti-gun columnist Mary
McGrory in an early 1978 article—which "although modest,

was what Shields was hoping for. It tightens standards for licensing gun dealers, imposes a waiting period for would-be purchasers, outlaws purchases by felons, mental incompetents and drug addicts, bans the manufacture and sale of 'Saturday Night Specials' and requires police and FBI clearance for 'second transfers' of handguns."

However, McGrory noted "what baffles Shields now is what Jimmy Carter is waiting for, the handgun control bill is on his desk. Nothing is happening."

And nothing did happen, as Shields later mused: "I still think we have the president with us. It is somebody's pragmatic view of politics that is holding us up." Very pragmatic indeed: Jimmy recognized how powerful the pro-gun vote was, and is, as even Shields acknowledged in a 1977 *People* magazine interview: "But for those who oppose [gun] control, it is the single most important issue—and they will go to the wall on it. That's why a liberal like Sen. Frank Church always votes against gun controls. Most elections in this country are decided by less than 10 percent of the electorate, and no politician wants to risk alienating that deciding vote." Sound advice, Pete—don't forget it.

As 1977 closed, NCCH was claiming 30,000 members with a $500,000 annual budget.

YEAR 5: 1978

In January, BATF Director Rex Davis informed NCCH that he had rejected a NCCH request that the BATF release data stating how many and what calibers of handguns were being produced by American firearm manufacturers. Although this data is required by the Gun Control Act to be reported to the BATF, it was expected to remain confidential, as firearm manufacturers don't want their competitors to know what their sales volume is for any particular caliber.

Following Davis' rejection, the NCCH successfully petitioned under the Freedom of Information Act that this information be released. NCCH retained the Washington law firm of Fried, Frank, Harris, Shriver and Kampelman to litigate its case. However, it was agreed that the information released would have to be at least a year old. This gave some protection to the manufacturers.

9

NCCH launched its "Victims of Handgun Violence Project" in March which informed the media each month how many Americans had been killed by handguns during that month. This project was fairly successful for NCCH during its first year, but the media finally tired of its failure to influence politicians and dropped reporting the data.

The "Handgun Body Count" was used by NCCH as a fund raiser, and several celebrities endorsed the project: Sen. Jacob Javits, Rep. Peter Rodino, Mrs. Robert (Ethel) Kennedy, Martin Luther King, Sr., and Sen Edward Kennedy, who signed the following note: "Until recently, only the gun owners have been organized to fight on Capitol Hill. Now the rest of us are getting together. I hope that you'll read the enclosed [NCCH] material and join us."

The May 8, 1978 *Newsweek* devoted a full-page column to Mrs. Jeanne Shields, in which she wrote one of the more intelligent utterances ever issued by a Gun Grabber: "The main adversaries of handgun control are members of the powerful and financially entrenched National Rifle Association, *macho men who don't understand the definition of a civilized society.*" Not even *one* of its 2 million membership, Jeanne?

In June the Gun Grabbers suffered a severe setback when both the House and Senate supported an amendment to cut $4.2 million from the BATF budget to curtail that agency's attempt to develop a complete computerized data bank containing the names and addresses of all American gun owners. The NCCH had urged Congress to reject the amendment, but they failed 61-31 in the Senate and 314-80 in the House. The Mouse had roared, but Congress heard only a squeak.

Despite its extensive lobbying for a major anti-gun bill, and one which the NCCH thought President Carter would support, the September NCCH newsletter noted: "Political advisors to the President apparently fear that his support for handgun control would jeopardize his political base in the South and among conservatives."

Because of the confusion resulting from the name similarities of the National Coalition to Ban Handguns (NCBH) and the National Council to Control Handguns (NCCH), the latter changed its name to Handgun Control, Inc. (HCI) in

November 1978. Another change dating from 1978 was the elevation of Pete Shields to chairman and leader. NCCH may have changed its name and chief officer, but it didn't change its goals. Its November newsletter noted: "We have formed a legislative task force which is now drafting comprehensive handgun control legislation which is both feasible and enforceable. Such legislation will include registration, licensing, stopping the flow of 'Saturday Night Specials' into society and insuring accountability and responsibility for those who own handguns and those who engage in their commerce. Thus, while many of us might prefer an outright ban of handguns, we are realistic enough to know that such a goal is unattainable in America today."

YEAR 6: 1979

By the Spring of 1979, the HCI leadership finally realized that their earlier hopes that Pres. Carter would support restrictive gun-control legislation were being shattered by the White House itself.

Although HCI had expected the president to mention his support for new gun controls in his State of the Union address, he didn't. Shortly thereafter, Carter withdrew the nomination of noted Gun Grabber Norval Morris to become director of the Law Enforcement Assistance Administration (LEAA). Morris, who had written *A Politician's Guide to Gun Control*, and in which he had supported the abolishment of individual handgun ownership, had been strenuously opposed by the gun lobby because of his anti-gun views.

By March the NCCH suffered another setback when the Treasury Department formally withdrew a set of proposed firearm regulations. At the urging of the anti-gunners, Treasury had proposed that each firearm have a unique serial number and require gun dealers to report gun thefts to the BATF. However, the gun lobby lobbied successfully against the department's adoption of these regulations.

Suffering from its Spring political setbacks, HCI's executive vice-president Charles Orasin said, "We've kept our approach at the factual level for too long. *Now we want to get emotional with this thing.*" Orasin was referring to HCI's monthly "Handgun Bodycount" program which was used along with its "Roll of Handgun Dead" newsletter to inform the media of the number of reported handgun homicides during any given month. Orasin said that his group had decided that if photographs of hungry children attract donations for overseas food programs, the stories of handgun victims might move the public to support gun control.

The White House snub sent HCI into the eager waiting arms of Sen. Edward Kennedy in early 1979 to tout HCI's gun legislation. Kennedy relished the praise he knew would come from the anti-gun constituency: "We feel Sen. Kennedy is the only person in the country right now who can push for controls," Orasin said. "He's not afraid of the NRA and he speaks out not only as a politician but as someone who has been victimized by handgun violence."

HCI felt that Kennedy's clout as Senate Judiciary Committee chairman, where most gun legislation is submitted, would enhance the strength of the gun-control movement. However, Kennedy's halo was slightly tarnished in early April when the Senate Ethics Committee ruled that Kennedy had acted improperly by writing fund-raising letters for HCI and NCBH on his official Senate stationery.

Despite these setbacks, in March HCI won a small victory when a federal court denied a request for a preliminary injunction by gun manufacturers to prevent the BATF from releasing confidential handgun production records. The gun manufacturers had to file the injunction after the Treasury Department (which governs the BATF) had decided to release the information in an out-of-court settlement to an HCI request that the data be made public. Originally, Treasury Secretary Michael Blumenthal had opposed release of the data, but anti-gun pressure from the White House changed his mind. A Justice Department spokesman involved in the suit candidly commented: "The manufacturers did supply us with this information in good faith with the assurance that it would never be revealed."

In the suit Shields argued that the data's release would aid anti-handgun groups in the legislative arena. Upon hearing of the court's denial, Citizens Committee for the Right to Keep and Bear Arms Public Affairs Director John Snyder said: "This episode is another instance of the Treasury Department assisting the anti-gun lobby by providing it with expertise and data—all at the taxpayer's expense."

By summer, HCI's hopes had picked up. The helpful Sen. Kennedy signed an HCI fund-raising letter dated August 7 in which he claimed: "When Congress returns from its summer recess, I will introduce comprehensive and reasonable legislation designed to reduce the mindless proliferation of handguns in America. I intend to make this legislation a top priority in the 96th Congress. . . ."

This bill, according to HCI Legislative Director Donald E. Fraher, would stop the manufacture, sale and importation of small handguns, require local police departments to verify the eligibility of handgun purchasers, and require that all handgun transfers take place through licensed dealers, require manufacturers to "keep track of their distribution of handguns, similar to the way automobile manufacturers keep records," require dealers to report the theft of firearms, and establish a federal Handgun Victim's Compensation program.

Kennedy was to have introduced the bill in August. However, according to a March 9, 1980 *Boston Globe Magazine* article, a "half-hour before his scheduled speech," Sen. Kennedy "called it off. A near shouting match ensued between irate Handgun Control, Inc. staffers and Kennedy aides." Kennedy hesitated because "some political friends, eyeing his presidential campaign, tried to dissuade the Senator from backing another losing 'liberal' cause," according to the *Globe*. Good old Teddy, always reliable.

In late 1979 HCI asked Congress to oppose a decision reached by U.S. negotiators to the Multilateral Trade Negotiations to reduce the import duty on handgun parts from 21 percent to 8.4 percent. Although Rep. Vanik introduced HR 5147 to reject the change, Congress ignored the bill.

Realizing that whatever limited impact they had on Congress was quickly vaporizing, late in the year HCI initiated its Handgun Control, Inc. Political Action Committee (HCI-PAC) to "stop the NRA from continuing its campaign of intimidation and fear. . . . A political force which will work *for* the election of those who support strong handgun control legislation. A political force which will work *against* those who

13

buckle under to the pressure of the NRA and vote against the majority's will."

HCI claimed its PAC was necessary because "So pervasive is their power [pro-gun PACs] that Congressmen, Senators and even the President of the United States fear for their own re-election in 1980 if they follow through on campaign promises for handgun control. Congress fears. The President fears. . . . That's why we decided to launch the [PAC] to stop the NRA from continuing its campaign of intimidation and fear." Thus, HCI's PAC was established "to serve notice to the NRA that its days of bullying, badgering and buying our political leaders are numbered."

YEAR 7: 1980

After much delay and consternation, HCI was gleeful to report in January that two weeks before the Hero of Chappaquidick had announced he was seeking the Democratic presidential nomination, he and Rep. Rodino had finally introduced their "Handgun Crime Control Act" (S. 1936) which HCI hyped as being "the most comprehensive measure ever brought before the Congress to stem handgun violence."

Gun Week editor Joe Tartaro condemned the bill, claiming it was "a simply incredible instrument . . . [Kennedy] had managed to incorporate almost every restrictive anti-gun legislative device ever contemplated into one package." Tartaro had good reason to criticize the bill, for it proposed: (a) to ban the manufacture of 'Saturday Night Specials,' (b) to require new handgun buyers to qualify for a "license to purchase," and (c) required manufacturers to keep track of who last had purchased one of their guns.

Following the introduction of S. 1936, Shields attempted to pressure the White House in supporting the bill. In a March letter, Shields quoted from a campaign promise by President Carter that he would support a new, tough control bill: "I favor registration of handguns, a ban on the sale of cheap handguns, reasonable licensing provisions including a waiting period. . . ."

After Shields told his supporters that as "we [have] learned that the White House feared that introducing a 'Carter' bill would hurt his chances for reelection," Shields urged his

65,000 members to write to the president and "ask Jimmy Carter to publicly reaffirm the commitment to handgun control he made in 1976. Ask him to make his campaign promise of 1976 a reality in 1980!" Sensing that he had little to gain—but much to lose—in supporting the bill, Carter ignored the Gun Grabbers' demands.

Finally realizing that both the Democrat-dominated Senate and House had no interest in bringing S. 1936 out of its political morgue, in April HCI began criticizing a pro-gun bill which had been introduced by Sen. McClure and Rep Volkmer. HCI wrote that pro-gunners had "cleverly duped" nearly 100 congressmen and some 40 senators into co-sponsoring the Federal Firearms Law Reform Act, and because "the bill is indeed dangerous" HCI was committed to mount both a lobbying and political-action program aimed at stopping this legislation and to let the public know which members of Congress were "captives of the NRA."

While the defenders of gun rights had "cleverly duped" a majority of the Democrat-controlled Senate and a third of the House (197 total co-sponsors), Shields claimed: "Congress is responding [to his anti-gun S. 1936]. The response was fantastic! Already we've doubled the number of legislators willing to support this bill." Shields was ecstatic that out of Rep. Tip O'Neill's Democrat-dominated Congress, some 60 congressmen had stampeded to stand up to be counted as an A-1 Gun Grabber.

But he wasn't finished with chastising the pro-gun congressmen.

While S. 1936 was showing signs of advanced rigor mortis, the opposing pro-gun bill was sailing through Congress, no thanks to Pete Shields. Ever mindful of keeping a high intellectual level to the gun-control debate, Shields wrote to his supporters warning that the pro-gun bill "poses a serious threat to each and every American's safety" and while pro-gunners have a "political pistol pointed to the head of every member of Congress. . . . These gun fanatics have been successfully blocked"—temporarily, as it turned out, however.

With its bill failing in Congress, in June HCI appealed to both the Republican and Democratic national conventions to adopt platforms condemning handguns. The Republican Platform Committee declined hearing at all from the handgun castigators, while the Democrats adopted the following resolutions: "The Democratic Party supports the enactment of federal legislation to strengthen the presently inadequate regulation of the manufacture, assembly, distribution and possession of handguns and to ban Saturday Night Specials."

During various primary and general elections, HCI-PAC donated heavily to over 50 anti-gun congressmen, including $1,000 to both Sen Ted Kennedy and Rep. John Anderson, who was campaigning for the Republican presidential nomination. Congressional candidates who have received funds from HCI-PAC are listed in this book's "Anti-Gun Politics Equals Big Money" chapter.

Following the shooting of singer John Lennon in December, HCI claimed that 10,000 people joined the organization alone during that month, which pushed its membership over 100,000.

YEAR 8: 1981

The March shooting of President Ronald Reagan gave a tremendous boost to the fortunes of HCI. As Shields wrote: "On Tuesday morning after the shooting, an emergency meeting was held to map out a campaign to build momentum for passage of a national handgun control law. The decision was made to launch an unprecedented advertising campaign to recruit a million-member letter-writing army. Handgun Control ads were immediately placed in *The New York Times*, *The Minneapolis Tribune* and *The Los Angeles Times*. The Handgun Control, Inc. direct mail campaign was doubled to reach five million households with news of our work. Plans were made for a demonstration at the Capitol."

That Wednesday morning, HCI held a press conference to outline its campaign plan. Chairman Shields calmly said: "Must we bury another President before our elected representatives pass a handgun control law? Handgun Control, Inc. intends to develop its own political war chest to defeat the gun advocates in the 1982 elections."

Following some free air time on CBS' "60 Minutes," HCI reported that "in the next week, eleven bags of mail" came to its offices. HCI claimed that its ads in 22 newspapers drew "over a quarter of a million" new supporters, thereby doubling its membership by late April."The shooting of the President had swung the momentum back to the handgun control movement," HCI's newsletter bragged.

HCI predicted that the House Judiciary Subcommittee on Crime later in the year would hold "the first hearings on the handgun control issue since 1975!"

When the city council of Morton Grove, Illinois was considering enacting an ordinance prohibiting residents from owning handguns, Shields was skeptical about its results. Originally, he believed a ban would stir up the gun owners to such an extent that they would vigorously oppose any type of firearm registration or licensing proposals. However, when he realized that if he didn't embrace the ban the media would ignore his group, Shields decided to support the ban as a symbol of "reasonable" gun control.

In July, Shields wrote to his fellow Gun Grabbers: "We must persuade this Congress to pass effective national handgun control legislation *or else change the make-up of the Congress by electing handgun control supporters in 1982.*" He also announced that one of his new goals was to recruit *"one million* to the cause of handgun control. . . . who will make this a priority issue when they pull the lever in the 1982 elections." Shields announced "we have set a goal. By March 30, 1982—the first anniversary of the assassination attempt on President Reagan—we want to have identified one million Americans—ONE MILLION STRONG FOR HANDGUN CONTROL." In August, HCI was claiming that its membership had become 451,000 strong.

To reach its first million, HCI decided to expand its "Students for Handgun Control" program by running full-page ads in 250 college newspapers. They believed "we can reach 43 percent of the college and university students, some 5 million people." It urged students to start HCI campus chapters, and claimed that the following schools were participating in its program: Amherst, Brandeis, Bryn Mawr, Carroll College, Columbia, U.C. Berkeley, UCLA, U.C. San Diego, U.C. Santa Barbara, U.C. Santa Cruz, U. of District of Columbia, Duke, George Washington U., Georgetown, Goshen College, Haverford, Harvard, U. of Illinois, U. of Nevada, S.U.

of New York, Niagara U., Penn State, U. of Penn., Princeton, St. John's College, St. Olaf College, Stanford, Washington, U. in St. Louis, Wesleyan, Western Wash. U., William & Mary and Yale.

During the year several anti-gun bills were introduced in Congress. In response to anti-gun bills introduced by normally pro-gun Sen. Thurmond to require a 3-week waiting period and Sen. Dole's indicated support for a bill establishing a federal waiting period, HCI's newsletter commented: "Handgun Control, Inc. is encouraged by the introduction of these bills, and we are prepared to work with their sponsors toward the eventual passage of responsible and comprehensive handgun control legislation."

Late in the year, Gun Grabber Judge Hortense Gabel of New York revealed that justice is not always blind. Judge Gabel ordered New Jersey businessman Ward Warren to pay $2,500 to the "National Coalition for Handgun Control." This penalty was issued after New York police stopped Mr. Warren for an alleged traffic violation. When Warren opened his glove box, out popped his handgun which was properly registered in his home state of New Jersey, but, as it was not registered with the NYPD, Warren was charged with unlawful carrying of a concealed pistol. Rather than imprisoning Mr. Warren, the Judge ordered him to contribute to a Washington, D.C. anti-gun group.

At year's end, HCI was claiming over 610,000 supporters.

YEAR 9: 1982

In a January 23 interview with the *Chicago Tribune*, Shields reflected on the wisdom of communities enacting handgun-ban ordinances similar to those of Morton Grove, Illinois. Shields warned:

"When you have local communities passing gun laws like this, and if after a year, two years, of having the law, they are not seen to have had any effect, then it has a negative effect on the whole question of national policy.

"I would not recommend such a [handgun ban] system as broad national legislation. The legislation we endorse and favor is a national licensing system. I'd rather like it done on a state-by-state licensing system. . .

18

"I'd have restrictive licensing rather than permissive licensing. You would have to prove a need. . . .

"I don't think there's a gun law that would have eliminated any specific crime, because we have too many weapons. . . ."

Despite what appeared to be a spectacular fund-raising year during 1981 following the shootings of President Reagan and Pope John-Paul II, by early 1982 it was clear that the Gun Grabbers' much ballyhooed prediction of "soon to come" anti-gun legislative victories was faulty.

To rekindle the sagging spirit of his followers, Shields waved a bloody flag in his February appeal letter:

"[F]ollowing the murder of John Lennon and the attempt on our President's life, the National Rifle Association once again is thumbing its nose at us!. . . .

"Now it wants to wipe off the books the relatively mild handgun control laws passed after the assassination of Martin Luther King, Jr. and Senator Robert F. Kennedy!

"Must we bury another President . . . before our elected representatives pass an effective national handgun control law?

"Just who the hell is running this country . . . Congress or the National Rifle Association?"

Shields told his supporters that HCI's goals were "not only to stop the [pro-gun] McClure-Volkmer bill, but [we] will go on the offensive—pushing for passage of the Kennedy-Rodino Bill" which would halt the manufacture and sale of 'Saturday Night Specials'" and "make tracing handgun ownership as quick and easy as automobile ownership."

Shields urged his members to ask their friends to join HCI, because: "There's power in numbers. That's the *only* way we can beat the gun nuts."

Although Shields had said in his January *Chicago Tribune* interview that he opposed the handgun ban in Morton grove, his position apparently changed within several weeks. This change was noticed in a legal (amicus curiae) brief that HCI had filed concerning the ban. In the brief, HCI's attorneys remarked that the ban was a "reasonable restriction . . . which is a significant step toward effective state and national handgun control."

The legal brief highlights Shields' true Gun Grabber

19

thoughts through his contention that the Second Amendment "would not prohibit Morton Grove's *reasonable* restrictions on the possession of handguns. The sole function of the Second Amendment is to protect well regulated state militias. The right to keep and bear arms is a collective, rather than individual, right. That right has always been held to be subject to reasonable limitations. . . . The Morton Grove ordinance is *sensibly* directed at preventing the worst firearms abuse cases." (My emphasis.)

Shortly after HCI filed its brief, *Reports from Washington* questioned Shield's true motives by observing: "HCI's position was also thrown in doubt last year when it changed its logo to a ban-the-handgun symbol similar to the used by NCBH. They have since changed it back."

In mid-year Shields realized that his anti-gun drive was faltering, it had almost even shifted into reverse: There had not been any congressional hearings on any of his bills.

Attempting to resuscitate his lethargic cause, Shields tried another Kennedy ploy, enticing Robert F. Kennedy, Jr. to sign a fund raising letter:

"Congress consistently fails to pass meaningful handgun control legislation because the pistol lobby mounts mean-spirited campaigns against any Senator or Congressman who dares to speak out for handgun control.

"But you and I can change that. Easily. The pistol lobby is puny compared to us—the bulk of Americans who support handgun control."

The soon-to-be convicted drug user then urged HCI supporters to send a "support gun control" postcard to their congressmen.

While Shields claims that he wants to ban only small handguns and allow those who have obtained police approval to possess a handgun, we only need to look at the unsuccessful 1982 anti-handgun Proposition 15 campaign in California to discover how deceptively Shields speaks to the public. In truth, he is a full- fledged Gun Grabber.

Although Shields was originally opposed to endorsing Proposition 15—which attempted to "freeze" the number of handguns in that state by forbidding any future manufacture or importation of handguns into that state—by September he had decided that he couldn't let the other anti-gun groups steal all the limelight, so he began supporting the handgun freeze measure.

Following the 1978 recommendation of his aides that HCI had to get "emotional" over the gun control controversy, Shields wasn't bashful about waging a bloody flag campaign in the state where his son Nick had been assassinated. In a September fund-raising appeal letter Shields wrote:

"Our opponents, the National Rifle Association and the handgun makers, have launched a massive multi-media blitz of their own to defeat Proposition 15. Handgun makers like Charter Arms—*who made the handgun used to kill John Lennon*—have given $10,000 to the drive. (My emphasis.)

"*If* Proposition 15 wins . . . not only will we have defeated the NRA, our victory could well be the linchpin for future handgun control victories in many more states throughout the country."

At the November elections, California voters rejected the Gun Grabbers tasteless bloody-flag waving shenanigans and voted 2-to-1 *against* the enactment of Proposition 15!

But the humiliating loss on Prop. 15 was just the tip of the iceberg: a series of embarrassing defeats came to NCCH that day: BOTH of the California Democratic senatorial and gubernatorial candidates who had been persuaded to endorse Prop. 15 were rejected by the voters.

Besides suffering political losses during 1982, HCI's financial fortunes also declined. HCI's total revenues fell 6 percent to $2.6 million.

YEAR 10: 1983

In early 1983 Shields was telling his alleged 700,000 followers that, "The National Rifle Association is once again thumbing its nose at us." He warned:

"Fresh from its victory in California—where it saw to the defeat of Proposition 15, the Handgun Violence Prevention Act—the NRA, backed by America's handgun makers, is actively at work on a massive campaign to actually repeal the few handgun control laws we have!

"How is that for a callous disregard for the will of the people—a will demonstrated in countless polls that prove the vast majority of Americans want some measure of handgun control! Just think. The NRA has gotten its selfish way for years. . . ."

Of course, the ideological logic of the Gun Grabber won't let him admit that a statewide California vote is a reasonably good indicator of the will of the people. Obviously Pious Pete just wants *his* own selfish way.

It's true that a vast majority of Americans want "some measure of handgun control." What Pete fails to understand from these polls is they reflect that the people *themselves* want control of their own firearms, they don't want Big Brother Shields to unilaterally disarm American citizens.

This is demonstrable from several recent elections: the 1976 vote in Massachusetts when the public voted 2-to-1 to reject banning the individual ownership of handguns, the statewide 1982 vote in California where the vox populi rejected a measure to prohibit the future manufacture and importation handguns into that state, and the 1982 votes in Nevada and New Hampshire where the people overwhelmingly approved state constitutional amendments protecting their right to possess firearms.

Shields fails to realize that he is leading a Don Quixote attack against the public, not criminals.

Shields' three major efforts for 1984 were (1) stop the Congress from enacting the pro-gun McClure-Volkmer "Firearms Owner Protection" bill; (2) entice Congress to adopt the anti-gun Kennedy-Rodino "Handgun Control Act;" and (3) boost HCI's membership to over one million dedicated Gun Grabbers through his new CAMPAIGN ONE MILLION STRONG project.

In March, HCI testified before the Massachusetts Joint Committee on Public safety in support of a bill to ban subnosed handguns in that state.

Following the April 17-23 "National Victim Rights Week," New York City Mayor Edward Koch gave an award to HCI Board Member, Odile Stern, for her efforts in support of handgun control.

In May Shields stumbled across a new scheme to keep his supporters awake. Realizing that HCI was impotent to seduce the Republican-controlled Senate into enacting new controls on handguns, Shields jumped on the bandwagon to ban "cop killer" bullets. This was his new twist to the old bait-and-switch sales pitch. If Congress isn't interested in controlling handguns, perhaps HCI could come in through the back door and cut handgun ownership by limiting the supply of bullets.

The Gun Grabbers have always been intrigued with the novel idea that they could humorously play off the pro-gunners' contention that "Guns don't kill people, people kill people." The anti-gunners wanted to alter this concept slightly by rewording it to read" "Guns don't kill people, bullets kill people."

With this intellectual breakthrough, the Gun Grabbers hoped that they could piggyback their idea onto a bill that had been introduced by U.S. Representative Mario Biaggi, who as a former New York City policeman had been wounded 10 times during his 23 years with the NYPD. Following a television program which revealed to the public, and to criminals as well, that certain types of Teflon-coated bullets (KTWs, named after former law-enforcement officers Kopsch, Turcus and Ward who designed the bullet) were capable of penetrating bullet-proof (really bullet resistant) vests worn by police, Biaggi introduced a bill to outlaw their ownership by the public.

In "deep appreciation for all that Handgun Control, Inc. is doing to help pass my bill (H.R. 953) to ban so-called 'cop killer bullets'—armor piercing handgun ammunition," Rep. Biaggi signed a fund-raising letter for HCI in May. Shields asked his supporters to send him $225,000 to finance a four-point lobbying plan to heighten HCI's visibility.

The plan was to:

"FIRST, Handgun Control's lobbyists will work to build a broad-based coalition of both liberal and conservative lawmakers who will agree to co-sponsor either the Senate or House version of the cop-killer bullet bill and will vote FOR the bill in its final form.

"SECOND, we will do our best to urge congressional leaders to hold committee hearings on both Moynihan and Biaggi bills so that we can bring law enforcement officers to Washington to testify in support of the bills. . . .

"THIRD, through advertisements, mail alerts, and public

relations work, we will expose the opponents of these bills, particularly the NRA. We will show the public that the NRA is more radical now than ever and that it is not simply a firearms-safety organization.

"FOURTH, working through our State Resources Bank, we will fight to pass legislation banning cop-killer bullets at the state level, as well as at the national level. Already eight states have banned this bullet."

Pro-gunners have been opposing the anti-KTW legislation because ballistics experts from the U.S. Departments of Justice and Treasury have testified before Congress that the bill's definition of armor-piercing ammo was too broad and would encompass millions of conventional rounds in its ban. They promised Congress that they would make an in-depth study to see if a concise definition could be formulated, but after more than a year's effort the government experts informed Congress that they couldn't develop a workable definition.

During a hearing before a House subcommittee in 1982, a Treasury Department expert testified that current bullet ban proposals "invariably include a wide range of ammunition commonly used for hunting, target shooting or other legitimate and long-established purposes."

In that same hearing, a Justice Department official said ". . . our continuing study of this issue revealed that there are serious flaws in the broad ban on armor-piercing handgun ammunition proposed in [the Moynihan-Biaggi bill]. Moreover, in certain handgun calibers, the effect of a ban on armor- piercing bullets would effectively deprive firearms owners of the use of their weapons by rendering illegal all presently available commercially manufactured ammunition."

Another important flaw in the anti-KTW bills is that they misdirect anti- crime activities from cracking down on the criminal misuse of firearms to searching out inanimate objects.

In mid-1983, HCI placed an ad in the *Washington Post* requesting funds for its anti-KTW campaign. However, when their ad hinted that they were assisting he "Metropolitan Police, District of Columbia (MPDC) Vest Fund," which was a group trying to raise $500,000 to buy 3,000 bullet-proof vests for D.C. police officers, attorneys for the MPDC sent a

24

letter to HCI demanding that HCI "cease and desist from any and all oral and/or written activities which in any way links your organization with the MPDC Vest Fund."

MPDC was upset with HCI because its ad read, in part: "America's police have started two drives—the first to raise money for armored vests for all policemen—the second to ban the cop-killer bullets the vests can't stop." The ad contained two solicitation coupons, one for funds for the vest fund, the other was to be mailed to the donor's congressman to urge his support for the anti-KTW bill.

MPDC's complaint letter said, "Your [HCI's] actions have given the public impression that your organization is somehow related to the MPDC Vest Fund, which is not true. Your activities have also given the appearance that the MPDC Vest Fund supports your political and/or legislative aims. This likewise is not true."

June 1983 saw the formation HCI's "The Chairman's Committee," open to those willing to contribute "a small amount" each month to the *Chairman's Action Fund*. Shields attempted to whip up the fervor of his followers by urging them to send a donation immediately because "handgun control is on the verge of happening across America." Why, "Only a couple of weeks ago in Broward County, Florida, the county commission voted into law a tough handgun control ordinance. This was the first such measure passed in the South in this decade. . . . And Handgun Control, Inc. played a key role in the victory." However, Shields didn't tell his cohort that the county later rescinded its ordinance after several local city councils voted they were "opting out" of the county ordinance, which was permissible under a special state law which give broad independence of "home rule" to municipal governments.

Shields told potential "Chairman's Committee" donors that he had four steps which the new committee would take to "make handgun control a reality in America." They were:

"FIRST, we will take part in an intensive candidate recruitment effort. We must begin—right away—finding concerned men and women who will become handgun control leaders in the Congress. . . . Handgun Control wants to provide them with briefing materials and organize our supporters so that we can back their candidacies as best we know how.

25

"SECOND, we will build Handgun Control's membership to the *one million mark.* There's political power in numbers. . . . And this powerful force can be mobilized not only to win local and state handgun control battles but to win at the polls in 1984.

"THIRD, we will expand our effort to educate every voter to the very real possibility that they, and their loved ones, could easily become another handgun statistic, and that they must act now to help stop America's handgun violence and crime.

"FOURTH, we will redouble our efforts to work with local and state citizen groups attempting to pass handgun control laws. Today, groups are forming in Washington, Florida, Virginia and Georgia. We must be in a position to help them all we can against the gun nuts.

Shields claimed HCI needed more donations because, "Just in 1982, Handgun Control spent over a million dollars to support state and local handgun control legislation, and an additional $107,000 in the political arena. Yet we must do more this year—and next."

In July, HCI reaffirmed its hidden desire to ban handguns when its attorneys filed before the U.S. Supreme Court an *amicus curiae* brief in support of Morton Grove, Illinois' ordinance which prohibits the individual ownership of handguns. That brief claims that the ordinance is a "significant step toward effective handgun regulation," and that: "There is nothing *unreasonable* about Morton Grove's decision to subject handguns to *relatively* strict control."

"To relatively strict control"—what 1984 Doublespeak for an outright ban!

In advance preparation for the 1984 congressional elections, in September 1983, HCI solicited its members to begin donating to its Political Action Committee early so that, *One,* HCI "can use all possible resources to help elect friends of handgun control. And *Two,* to intensify our lobbying effort so that we can convince still more lawmakers on Capitol Hill that a federal handgun control law is the best way to dramatically lower the number of Americans who are felled each and every year with killer handguns."

In recognizing the power of pro-gun PACs, Shields conceded their usefulness:

"In the coming election year, Handgun Control, Inc. must take a page out of the NRA's book.

"Now, I don't mean that we will attack our opponents with smear tactics, the way the NRA does.

"It's just that in races important to HCI, I intend to concede absolutely nothing to the National Rifle Association.

"And that's why I'm writing to you personally today to announce the immediate launching of our VICTORY-84 CAMPAIGN."

Shields apparently feels that getting into political campaigns soils HCI's image: "IF we at Handgun Control had a choice about whether or not to continue our political action committee, we might well choose to get out of the PAC business." But, Shields just couldn't break HCI away from its PAC; "we simply have no choice.Not when our opponents will spend millions to acquire a pro-gun Congress. Millions to put NRA yes-men in office."

While Shields has written letters questioning "Just who the hell is running this country: Congress or the National Rifle Association?," apparently he feels it's okay for anti-gun no-men to run Congress.

The hypocrisy of Pious Pete's inconsistency in condemning pro-gun PACs while maintaining his own was recognized even by a prestigious *Congressional Quarterly* researcher, who wrote:

"[The anti-gun PACs] propose to counter the NRA by doing precisely what the NRA has done so successfully for years— collecting as much money as it can from members, then using it to support candidates who agree with its views. . . .

"The difference between [anti-gun PACs] and the NRA is that the NRA will have much more money to spend. . . . Does that make the NRA more suspect as a pressure group? Should the size of a PAC's bankroll be the line that separate legitimate lobbying from charges of improperly buying votes with campaign cash?

"There is . . . a *curious logic* at work when other interest groups decry the political influence of their adversaries and then attempt to duplicate that clout by the same means."

Shields set a goal of raising $500,000 in PAC dollars for the 1984 elections. About half of that amount is earmarked for

senate and congressional primary and general elections, with
the remaining being allocated for voter education campaigns,
candidate briefing materials, voter information about presidential candidates' stands on handgun control, contributions
to help establish handgun- control PACs in the states, and for
HCI to make presentations at candidate forums, before
Democratic and Republican Platform Committees, and for
work at these parties' national conventions.

In October 1983 hearings before a Senate subcommittee on
the pro-gun McClure-Volkmer bill, Shields testified against
the bill, claiming that it "would lift the current prohibition on
mail-order gun sales." Shields told the senators that the rifle
used by Lee Harvey Oswald (an American turncoat who received arms training in Russia) to kill President Kennedy had
been ordered through the mail, and that the revolver used by
Oswald to kill Dallas Patrolman Tippit had been obtained
from a mail-order ad clipped from an issue of the NRA's
American Rifleman.

Following his testimony, Shields mailed a letter to his
followers and urged them to mail their congressmen an HCI-
prepared postcard which tastelessly bore a photograph of
Pres. Kennedy along with the comment: "The McClure-
Volkmer Gun Decontrol Bill is dangerous and wrong.We
should make it harder, not easier, for potential assassins and
criminals to get guns."

YEAR 11: 1984

Early in 1984 HCI rushed to mail its ONE MILLION STRONG
package, and asked its 815,992 supporters to sign up a friend
to help HCI reach a million members "by March 30, 1984—
the third anniversary of the attempt on President Reagan's
life." As Shields told his followers, "We must have that mil-
lion-supporter clout if we are to defeat once and for all the
NRA's deadly McClure-Volkmer Gun Decontrol Bill. This
bill would (1) *reinstate* mail-order gun sales; and (2) virtually
destroy the 1968 Gun Control Act."

With a million members financing HCI, Shields could then
(1) produce a new handgun-control film "which will be aired
this year on television stations across America," (2) launch
"the most massive direct mail recruitment program in our

history. In the first three months of '84 alone we hope to mail more than 3,500,000 letters to Americans who, research shows, may well be sympathetic to our cause," and (3) "build on recent political and legal victories over the NRA—and have these victories reported by the media—so that more people will come to understand how much clout HCI has gained on Capitol Hill."

Also early in the year, in response to the fact that handgun manufacturers had contributed heavily during late 1982 to defeat the anti-gun Prop. 15 measure in California, HCI began a mudslinging campaign against handgun manufacturers: HCI was out to get the "MERCHANTS OF DEATH." HCI started off its 1984 terror campaign through a column by HCI staffer Barbara Lautman, which appeared in the Hinesville, Georgia, *Coastal Courier*. In her diatribe, Lautman wrote:

Today, we have the New Merchants of Death . . . The National Rifle Association has long been in the forefront of efforts to repeal existing gun laws and prevent new laws from being enacted, but few realize that it is the power of the gun makers, the NRA's silent partner, that provides the financial backing necessary to carry on this fight. . . .

"To the gun makers, promoting the unrestricted sale and ownership of handguns is just good business. They don;'t consider the 20,000 Americans who each year are killed with their products. They don't care about the 250,000 others who are raped, robbed, threatened or assaulted with handguns. The gun makers are concerned with profit. . . .

"So instead of taking a rational position on the issue, the gun makers continue to hide behind the lobbying power of the NRA. Occasionally they get smoked out as they did in California during the Proposition 15 campaign when the handgun industry contributed one million dollars to see that the initiative was defeated.

"The situation is the same on the federal level. Rather than use their millions to promote handgun safety and reasonable controls, the gun makers finance campaigns to fight such proposals. . . .

"So it is by no means unfair or harsh to say that the gun makers are the New Merchants of Death. . . ."

The language of this letter was mild compared to the vitriolic one penned by Shields himself. In an early February letter to this friends, Shields *calmly* wrote:

"That's right. A group of total strangers *is* willing to see you or a friend or loved one killed or injured. There's nothing personal in it. They're not out to get you. All they want is more profit. . . .

"You call it cold-blooded. They call it good business.

"'They' are the innumerable private companies in America, large and small, that manufacture handguns.

"And they wouldn't lost a minute's sleep if you or a member of your family were blown away tonight on a street in your hometown—just as long as they make a couple of bucks from the handgun used to do it.

"These handgun makers have become America's new 'Merchants of Death.' "

Pete Shields has become America's foremost "Mudslinging Gun Grabber of the Decade" candidate—and he wonders why his group has been impotent in Congress.

In mid-June 1984, Pete Shields circulated his Board of Directors new "Five Year Plan" which will "marshal the resources of our organization behind a rational course of action that will take HANDGUN CONTROL *beyond* the National Rifle Association, both in size and in power." And his strategy?

Part I: A massive recruitment drive to become TWO MILLION STRONG by March 30, 1985.

Part II: Organize our supporters who live in the home districts of those members of Congress whose votes we must win if we are to pass the federal handgun-control law that we want.

Part III: Write, procure, and distribute a half-hour television program made for the express purpose of recruiting new supporters, and

Part IV: Implement an intensive lobbying plan which we have devised to improve the climate for handgun-control legislation on Capitol Hill.

While HCI was preparing to kick off its new membership drive—but like Lucy pulling the football away from Charlie Brown before he is able to kick it at the start of each new football season—the federal government pulled the rug out from under HCI.

30

On July 16, the Federal Elections Commission fined the Handgun Control, Inc. Political Action Committee (HCI-PAC) $15,000 for illegal solicitation of funds.

Specifically, the "Commission has determined that respondents [HCI-PAC] violated [federal elections law] by soliciting contributions to HCI-PAC from individuals who do not constitute members of HCI within the meaning of the Federal Elections Campaign Act of 1971. . . .

"For purposes of settling this matter . . . respondents will pay a civil penalty in the amount of $15,000 to the U.S. Treasurer . . . and HCI is to change its membership requirements."

The FEC action was a "Conciliation Agreement" (MUR-1604) whereby the accused acknowledge their violations and agree to adhere to FEC regulations. Charles Orasin, executive vice-president of HCI and treasurer of HCI-PAC, signed the agreement on July 10. The FEC approved it on July 16, 1984.

HCI-PAC solicits contributions for distribution to anti-gun federal congressional candidates. [See Chapter 5.]

It's interesting to note the irony that while HCI leader Nelson "Pete" Shields constantly accuses pro-gunners of "buying" congressional support, it was his group that was fined for illegal campaign practices.

Eight days after having his knuckles rapped by the FEC, Shields mailed a fund-raising letter in which—instead of acknowledging his unethical electioneering practices—he sent up a smoke screen by claiming that "through slick legal maneuvers and political harassment the NRA is trying to shut us down" by "the NRA using *its friends* at the Federal Elections Commission to close down our political fund."

Apparently, Pious Pete has been reading so many of his own fund-raising letters he really believes that somehow the pro-gun movement controls the entire Federal Elections Commission. Pete, you simply got caught violating federal election law.

Are we to see any reasonable and rational anti-crime recommendations from HCI? Probably not, for as Shields has claimed in one of this flyers: "Whether it takes one year, five years, or ten years, Handgun Control, Inc. will never give up. . . . We're here to stay."

Second Fiddle:
The National Coalition
to Ban Handguns

THE NATIONAL COALITION TO BAN HANDGUNS (NCBH), head-quartered in Washington, D.C., is another 'Gun Grabber Biggie,' second only to Handgun Control, Inc. in size and irrationality. NCBH has striven to sell your rights down the river just as hard as HCI, but for a number of reasons never attracted as much money or as many members. Nevertheless, it ranks up there with the worst of the coercive utopians. NCBH has at times worked on the same projects as HCI, mostly by coincidence or because one couldn't let the other steal its Gun Grabbing thunder. For that reason, some of NCBH's story will retrace the steps of HCI we followed in the first chapter.

The goals of NCBH have been clearly set forth in its literature; it is "An alliance of religious and educational organizations, citizen and public interest groups, professional societies and other associations, the National Coalition to Ban Handguns is engaging in a vigorous campaign to change the country's mood, and to increase the 41 percent of the American people who favor outright banning of handguns to over 70 percent. Then, we believe, the Congress will act in a firm, meaningful way."

National Coalition to Ban Handguns Executive Director Michael Beard identifies the objectives of the NCBH as the "banning of handguns from importation, manufacture, sale, transfer, possession and use in U.S. society except for limited uses such as the military, police, security guards and pistol clubs (with guns kept safely on the club's premises)." Gun dealers would also be permitted to trade in antique weapons kept and sold in unfireable condition.

The NCBH notes, "Assisting national, state, and local groups working to ban handguns is an important purpose of the Coalition. The national organization relates to such groups helping them to work with their constituencies and to share materials, audio-visuals, and other information and resources. The NCBH also engages in research, develops original materials, relates to the media, and undertakes field work assignments."

In late 1976, the NCBH conceded: "The Board of Church and Society of the United Methodist Church is the fiscal agent for the Coalition, and is responsible for all business matters." This changed in 1976, following a complaint filed by the Citizens Committee for the Right to Keep and Bear Arms, when CCRKBA wrote to the IRS and objected that it was improper for the Church to share its tax-exempt privileges with the NCBH. In late 1976, the IRS agreed and the two groups separated.

According to a *Washington Star* article, Mike Beard said of CCRKBA's complaint: "It nearly made us go bankrupt. For six months during the IRS investigation we couldn't raise funds. The IRS said we couldn't tell anyone funds were tax deductible. But it has forced us to become political, since we no longer have the church's tax privilege. We'll have to lobby on the Hill now to show our side."

Concerning 'Saturday Night Special' handguns, NCBH maintains that as "the definition of such weapons is practically impossible," all handguns should be prohibited. Otherwise, as an August 1976 flyer warned, "If they are defined as guns with barrels of 6 inches or less, then manufacturers could easily produce gun barrels of 6½ inches. A 'Saturday Night Special' ban would probably be circumventable."

NCBH contends that a total handgun ban is needed:

"Considering the critical nature of the problem, the Coalition does not believe at anything less than banning handguns provides an adequate solution at this juncture of U.S. history. Imposing penalties, registration and licensing, outlawing 'Saturday Night Specials' would all be very limited and modest steps—even taken together—toward coping with the very serious problem handguns present in America.

"Registration could identify a weapon used in a murder (if you could find the weapon) but only after the crime had already been committed.

"Outlawing the sale of 'Saturday Night Specials' would deal only with a small percentage of murders and other crimes.

"Licensing would not screen out those who commit crimes of passion since such persons, generally speaking, have not previously been convicted of a serious offense."

One factor which strongly influenced Michael Beard's drive to ban handguns was reported in the August 1981 edition of the Japanese *Playboy* magazine: "Beard told the audience how he vowed never to fool around with a gun after seeing a friend of his killing himself while playing with his father's gun when he was nine years old." This revelation came during a gun- control symposium featuring Beard and NRA's Aquilino, which had been sponsored by the CloseUp Foundation, a national high school education group, in 1981 in Washington, D.C.

In early 1976, NCBH listed on its stationery that the following organizations were supportive of its efforts:

Participating Organizations
American Ethical Union
Americans for Democratic Action
Board of Church and Society, United Methodist Church
Center for Social Action, United Church of Christ
Church of the Brethren, Washington Office
Friends Committee on National Legislation
International Ladies' Garment Workers' Union
Jesuit Conference, Office of Social Ministries
National Alliance for Safer Cities
National Association of Social Workers
National Council of Jewish Women, Inc.
National Council of Negro Women
The Program Agency, United Presbyterian Church in the U.S.A.
Union of American Hebrew Congregations
Unitarian Universalist Association, Washington Office for Social Concern

United Synagogue of America

National Advisory Council

Bishop James Armstrong   John Kenneth Galbraith
Leonard Bernstein   Rep. Michael Harrington
Eugene Carson Blacke   Rabbi Benjamin Z. Kreitman
Julian Bond   Norman Lear
Rabbi Balfour Brickner   Bishop James K. Matthews
Harvey Cox   Otto Preminger
Helen Gahagan Douglas   Rabbi Stanley Rabinowitz
Bishop Carroll Dozier   William P. Thompson
Rep. Robert Drinan   Albert Vorspan
James Farmer   Roy Wilkins
Rep. Walter Fauntroy

Executive Committee

Robert Alpern (Unitarian Universalist Assoc.)
Nick Brock (Friends Committee on National Legislation)
Jack Corbett, NCBH Chairperson (Board of Church and Society, United Methodist Church
Evelyn Dubrow (International Ladies' Garment Workers' Union)
Sylvia Eller
Al Gonzales
James Green
Howard Maxwell
Robert McAlpine (National Urban League)
Kathleen Miller (Legislative representative for ACLU)
Susan Rubin (American Jewish Committee)
Barbara Stolz

In a typical fund-appeal letter, Executive Director Michael Beard warned of the dangers of the pro-gun movement:

"While the gun lobby spreads its false statements—there is no Constitutional right to carry guns—and works its will against the overwhelming majority of Americans who want some kind of strong handgun control, the savagery goes on. . . .

"If two-thirds of the American people want tough handgun control laws, why don't we have them: Because the gun industry is a multi-billion dollar business which, along with the gun lobby, is prepared to spend vast sums of money to discourage Congress from enacting any meaningful firearms legislation. So far, the pro-gun interests and their dollars have far outweighed public opinion."

So what did Beard promise his contributors that NCBH would do to counter the pro-gunners?:

"We're taking the actions that must be taken to banish handguns, including distributing literature and films to local and national groups, organizing public meetings, supporting the efforts of local gun control committees, providing speakers, initiating gun victim's' press conferences, presenting the facts and pointing out fallacies to the radio, television and print media."

Therefore, Beard humorously asks: "You may want to consider contributing the price of a 'Saturday Night Special'—$25.00—to help eliminate a 'Saturday Night Special'."

By late 1976, the NCBH staff consisted of: Michael Beard, executive director; Jack Corbett, chairperson; and Sol Rubin, vice chairperson.

In October, the National Gun Control Center (HGCC had offices in both Montgomery, Alabama and Washington, D.C.) decided to merge with the NCBH. Beard said the action brought "together about 43,000 handgun control supporters nationwide." As NGCC Executive Secretary Michael Fidlow explained the consolidation: "NCBH leaders have been active in gun control for more than 10 years; the Coalition has recently accelerated its activities in the area of public education . . . This action is not the end of the GCC's efforts, but the beginning of a more powerful coalition . . . At a time when the gun control movement is building momentum, the last thing we want or can afford is unnecessary duplication of effort."

NCBH, and the entire Gun Grabber movement suffered their most humiliating defeat on November 2, 1976, when Massachusetts voters rejected by 2-to-1 a referendum measure (Question 5) which sought to ban the individual ownership of handguns.

Undaunted by the voice of the people, late in the year

NCBH began publishing its bi-monthly *Handgun Control News* newsletter.

One cannot but wonder about the true intentions of NCBH. Are they merely interested in banning handguns as a means to reduce crime, or instead, do its directors secretly desire banning rifles and shotguns also?

Michael Beard in his Dec. 1976/Jan. 1977 newsletter claimed that "The groups now working on the national scene for handgun control have publicly stated that they are not opposed to the legitimate use of long guns. Rifles and shotguns are used for criminal purposes much less frequently than are handguns. Rifle and shotguns do have legitimate uses. But the handgun exists only to kill."

However is NCBH really interested in banning only handguns? It wouldn't appear so according to NCBH Communications Director Susan Love, who made the following remark on Nov. 6, 1977 during a debate at Johns Hopkins University: "We didn't go after the long gun because we don't want all those hunters on our back." Out of the mouths of babes. . . .

NCBH supports the Washington, D.C. handgun ban which also made it illegal to have a loaded rifle in your home. In a debate I had with Michael Beard on Seattle's KING-TV I made this point. The host of the show asked Michael "You live in Washington, D.C. What do you use for self-defense?" He replied, "A pool cue." The next time we debated on television, I wore a button saying BAN POOL CUES.

SURVIVAL DAYS

Early in 1977, NCBH began its "Survival Days" project (May 20-22), whereby they coordinated with several ministers in four target cities (Atlanta, New York, Chicago and San Francisco) and asked them to request that their congregations surrender their handguns to them for eventual destruction. The NCBH mailed out details of its "Survival Days" project to 5,000 churches and synagogues in those four cities.

NCBH claimed that 1,200 churches and synagogues participated in the project, and that 73 handguns were turned in following an appeal to do so by their minister. NCBH said its project was endorsed by Mayors Jackson of Atlanta, Moscone of San Francisco and Acting Mayor Bilandic of Chicago, all of whom "issued official statements proclaiming Mar 20-22 as Survival Days and urging citizens to participate in the programs."

In Atlanta, "a special children's toy gun turn-in was conducted prior to Survival Days week at Ebenezer Baptist Church where Rev. Martin Luther King, Sr. is Pastor."

The Illinois Rifle Association sought to call a halt to the program in Chicago through a lawsuit by claiming that it was in violation of state law. However, Circuit Court Judge Joseph Wosik ruled in favor of the city's co-sponsorship by saying, "If one life is saved, this program will be a success."

Although the NCBH had initially convinced the U.S. Bureau of Alcohol, Tobacco and Firearms to agree to be the "official collection agent" for the soon-to- be surrendered guns, on May 20 Treasury Department Deputy Assistant for Enforcement, James Featherstone, issued an order to BATF field agents and informed them that they could not collect and destroy the weapons. Local police picked up the guns instead.

In early 1977, NCBH hired Sam Fields to become its Field Director. Previously, Fields had been senior lobbyist for the Americans For Democratic Action, where he specialized in tax and health matters. His new NCBH job was to organize new state and city anti-handgun groups and make local media appearances.

In April, the following individuals were elected to NCBH's

Executive Committee

Robert Alpern (Unitarian Universalist Assoc.)

Nick Brock (Friends Committee on National Legislation)

Jack Corbett. (NCBH Chairperson before 1977; Board of Church and Society, United Methodist Church.

Evelyn Dubrow (International Ladies' Garment Workers' Union)

David Gorin (American Jewish Congress)

Robert McAlpine (National Urban League)

Kay McGrath (Women's National Democratic Club-PAC)

Howard C. Maxwell (The Program Agency, United Presbyterian Church in the U.S.A.)

Kathleen Miller (NCBH Chairperson and Legislative representative for ACLU)
Louise Milone (B'nai B'rith Women)
Susan Rubin (American Jewish Committee)

Staff:
Kathleen Miller, NCBH Chairperson (replaced Jack Corbett)
David Gorin, NCBH Vice-chairperson (D.C. representative for American Jewish Congress)
Robert Alpern, Secretary/Treasurer (D.C. Director of the Unitarian Universalist Association)

One of the major "achievements" of NCBH during 1977 was to file a complaint against an NRA display booth at Expo '77, which was held in Washington, D.C. The outcome was that NRA removed its exhibit. As NCBH's newsletter described this stupendous feat:

"The NCBH, in anticipation of the NRA's political activity at the fair, had written that the NRA display would be inconsistent with the theme of the fair and its exhibits.

"NCBH's executive director, Michael Beard, had contended that the NRA booth would contain 'considerable . . . provocative material devoted to proliferating America's number one murder weapon, handguns. . . .'

"The Capitol Centre had an agreement with the NRA concerning what would be distributed and displayed at Expo '77. When it came to the attention of Centre officials that the NRA was violating that agreement, the officials demanded the removal of the politically-oriented components of the display. However, since such posters, etc. comprised the major part of its display, the NRA removed the entire exhibit."

In mid-1977 NCBH stated that the following groups were NCBH "Participating Organizations:"

American Civil Liberties Union
American Ethical Union
American Jewish Committee
American Jewish Congress

Americans for Democratic Action
Board of Church and Society, United Methodist Church
B'nai B'rith Women
Center for Social Action, United Church of Christ
Department of Social Development and World Peace, U.S. Catholic Conference
Disarm Educational Fund
Friends Committee on National Legislation
International Ladies' Garment Workers' Union
Jesuit Conference, Office of Social Ministries
National Alliance for Safer Cities
National Association of Social Workers
National Council of Jewish Women, Inc.
National Council of Negro Women
National Jewish Welfare Board
Political Action Committee, Women's National Democratic Club
The Program Agency, United Presbyterian Church in the U.S.A.
Union of American Hebrew Congregations
United Synagogue of America Women's Division, Board of Global Ministries, United Methodist Church
Women's League for Conservative Judaism
Young Women's Christian Association of the U.S.A. National Board

In another publication, "NCBH, What It Is and What It Does," NCBH listed the following groups as "participating organizations:"

American Civil Liberties Union
Americans for Democratic Action
Committee for the Study of Handgun Misuse
National Education Association
Unitarian Universalist Association

In an NCBH publication, "Twenty questions and answers," which was circulated in 1978, the following comments about 'Saturday Night Special' handguns and registration were made:

"15. Q: Isn't registration of handguns the answer?

A: It is doubtful that registration would act as a sufficient deterrent. Criminals do not leave their guns behind to be traced, now would they register them in the first place. . . . By itself, registration is an insufficient response.

"16. Q: Wouldn't outlawing the sale of 'Saturday Night Special' handguns help solve the problem?

A: No. The 'Saturday Night Special' represents only about 22 percent of the handguns sold. A 'Saturday Night Special' ban would easily be circumvented."

With the election of Jimmy Carter to the White House, the 35-year-old Beard predicted in February 1978: "We expect the administration to introduce next month a fairly comprehensive gun control bill—and we expect it to pass, if not this year, then certainly in 1979." Beard hoped to accomplish this with his group's $200,000 annual budget and 75,000 contributors.

The Feb. 15 *Seattle Times* quoted Beard during a tour of Western States as saying: " 'We don't labor under any myth that it (a handgun bill) will reduce crime,' said Beard, 'But it will reduce death from crimes of passion, accidents and suicide.' " The *Seattle Times* also wrote, "The possession, manufacture, sale and transfer of private handguns will be prohibited in the United States within five years, the executive director of the National Coalition to Ban Handguns predicted here Monday."

During May, House Judiciary's Subcommittee on Crime hearings, Beard testified in support of a proposed new BATF regulation which would have improved the means for the bureau to trace registered guns.

NCBH revealed in mid-year that the following organizations had joined as a "participating organization:"

American Psychiatric Association
American Public Health Association
Black Women's Community Development Foundation
Church of the Brethren, Washington, D.C. Office
United Universalist Association

U.S. Conference of Mayors
U.S. National Student Association

In August the NCBH convinced Sen. Edward Kennedy to sign a fund- raising letter for them. This pillar of Taxachusetts wrote: "Now we have the National Coalition to Ban Handguns, made up of over thirty religious and lay groups cutting across the full spectrum of American public opinion. NCBH has assumed the formidable task of organizing this majority into an effective vehicle for firearms control."

In an accompanying letter, Beard moaned:
"[T]he NRA and other pro-gun groups have opposed every effort on every level to enact legislation that could reduce the bloodbath.

"They have flooded America with distorted, inaccurate information and false slogans. . . . They have attacked elected officials and candidates who favor handgun control . . . they have instigated and orchestrated the most vicious letter-writing campaigns, directed against clergymen and Presidents, judges and Senators, and especially against organizations like the National Coalition to Ban Handguns. . . .

"Two years ago, the right-wing Citizens Committee for the Right to Keep and Bear Arms called on the IRS to revoke the tax-exempt status enjoyed by one of our sponsoring organizations. . . .

"We have recently initiated a lawsuit challenging a federal statute that requires the U.S. Army to sell surplus weapons, at discount prices, *only* to dues-paying members of the National Rifle Association.

"This statute, which put millions of dollars into NRA coffers and subsidizes their misguided campaign against handgun control, requires any citizen who wants to take advantage of a government benefit to give money to an organization whose purposes and program he or she may oppose. . . ."

(The question arises, who is it that would oppose the NRA and at the same time want to buy a firearm? Evidently, common-sense logic is not one of the strong points of the Gun Grabbers.)

Beard went on:

43

"We're working to enlist *a million* concerned Americans in support of the Coalition, to carry our anti-handgun-abuse message across the land with incontrovertible evidence and impassioned logic. A million people who will demonstrate to our elected officials that a vote *for* handgun control is not political suicide."

(Now we get it: *impassioned* logic—whatever that is—drives the mental functions of the Gun Grabbers. Fortunately, our engineers, scientists and brain surgeons avoid it.)

While prior NCBH literature has claimed that "long guns are valid sporting arms," in August, Field Director Sam Fields found it necessary to complain about some forms of pro-long gun activities. He appeared before the U.S. Fish and Wildlife Service to supposedly "document charges that Maine state official in concert with the National Rifle Association have been using federal dollars to illegally purchase and distribute political propaganda through the state Hunter Education Program."

Fields told the Service that ". . . we emphatically believe that such (hunter safety) courses should not be used for political propagandizing or legislative lobbying."

Fields was complaining about a sentence in a Maine manual which read: "Guns themselves are not dangerous . . . approach firearms for the safe, recreation objects they really are, like fine golf clubs." Some "propagandizing"!

He also complained about Maine's purchase of $1,125 of NRA patches, which were distributed to the course members. Fields said this turned 6,000 Maine residents "into walking billboards for the NRA."

During this same era of significant NCBH action, Catherine Chodrow became NCBH's communications director.

QUESTIONNAIRE TIME

One creative project of the NCBH was to develop a "Handgun Control Questionnaire" which it requested its members to mail to their local congressional candidates and ask them to report to the NCBH whether they supported: banning the sale of small handguns; banning the ownership of handguns; or registering all handguns.

In starting off 1979, on January 24, Michael Beard, Rep. Abner Mikva and Mayor Diane Feinstein of San Francisco held a propaganda conference in Washington, D.C. and asked President Carter to live up to his 1976 campaign promise to strengthen federal gun-control laws.

Shortly thereafter, NCBH announced that Vice-chairperson Howard Maxwell had succeeded retiring Chairperson Kathleen Miller. Maxwell was a representative of the Program Agency of the United Presbyterian Church in the U.S.A. In mid-year, Maxwell was replaced by J. Elliott Corbett, and Susan Love became editor of *Handgun Control News*.

In April the NCBH was dealt an embarrassing public-relations blow when the U.S. Senate Select Ethics Committee voted 3 to 0 that Sen. Edward Kennedy acted improperly by writing fund-raising letters for NCBH—and Handgun Control, Inc., as described in Chapter One.

Here's what the committee actually ruled:

"In the opinion of the Select Committee that it is improper conduct which reflects upon the Senate for a Senator to authorize or allow a non-senate individual, group or organization to use the words 'United States Senate' and 'Official Business,' or any combination thereof, on any letterhead or envelope."

The committee issued its decision following a complaint filed by CCRKBA chief lobbyist John M. Snyder, who wrote in his complaint, "Since the United States Senate, following the recommendation of its Select Committee on Ethics, has prohibited its Members from using its official Senate stationery for private organizations' fund raising purposes, we hereby file this formal complaint with your Committee, protesting this public, double-barrelled thwarting of the official ethics of the Senate."

NCBH v. NRA

NCBH scored a judicial victory over the NRA when on September 4 federal Judge Harold Greene found in favor of an NCBH lawsuit [Gavett v..Alexander] and overturned a 55-year-old federal law that required NRA membership for the purchase of surplus military rifles. With NRA mem-

45

bership, and by participating in an NRA-sponsored marksmanship course, a participant had been enabled by statute to
purchase—at discount prices—surplus military firearms, primarily M-1 carbines, from the U.S. Department of Civilian
Marksmanship Program (DCM). The NCBH filed the lawsuit in
November 1978 in an attempt to undermine membership in the
NRA. NCBH reasoned that if individuals could obtain the
highly prized military rifles without needing to join the NRA,
perhaps a significant number would let their membership lapse.

As Beard said of his devious deed: "We are gratified that
the courts have sought to remedy this injustice; my only
regret is that it was not done twenty years ago. Had it been
accomplished in the 1950s, NRA power would have been
curtailed and handgun control a reality."

While some gun owners may feel that this "victory" is of
miniscule importance, an NCBH editorial explained its long-
range threatening implications and future tactics of the Gun
Grabbers:

"Why? Because it proves the importance of fighting for
handgun control on many different levels. It is not enough to
concentrate solely on getting a national handgun control law
passed by the U.S. Congress. . . . So handgun control activists must fight many other more minor skirmishes where
victories are more readily attainable. And these victories will
eventually make that goal of a national law a reality. . . .

"Therefore any campaigns to secure enactment of laws on
the state and local level; any programs, such as handgun
turn-in drives which draw attention to the severity of the
handgun violence problem; any attempts to reduce the power
of the gun lobby are vitally important and must be undertaken and continued. Let's face it, morale is crucial to any
movement, and winning a small battle is better then not
winning any at all."

A week after this court victory, Beard still felt chipper
enough at a national conference on handgun control to boast
that NCBH was going to sue the NRA at every turn and
clucked: "We've got more suits now than Brooks Brothers
does." The conference in Washington, D.C. had been sponsored by the Handgun Control Staff of the U.S. Conference of
Mayors.

This court decision so mesmerized Beard that he was still gloating over it in an October fund-raising letter: "Now we've got the NRA where we want them, and beating *them* in court is like shooting fish in a barrel!" Remember safety, Michael, never shoot into water: the shots have a tendency to ricochet elsewhere than at your intended target.

This gambit almost backfired against the NCBH. To implement the lawsuit, Fields, a resident of Washington, D.C., travelled to Wheaton, Maryland, to meet with co-plaintiff Geoffrey Gavett. There they purchased a rifle which Fields took back to Washington, D.C. A pro-gun congressman maintained that this was a violation of the federal Gun Control Act, and he asked the U.S. Justice Department to investigate the questionable transaction.

On August 27, Philip B. Heyman, assistant attorney general for the Criminal Division of the Justice Department, opined to the congressman:

"You cited the transcript of a deposition by Geoffrey Gavett taken on March 30, 1979, as indicating that Gavett committed a violation of 18 USC 922(A)(5) and Sam Fields, an employee of the National Coalition to Ban Handguns committed a violation of the same statute and also a violation of 18 USC 922(a)(3).

"You also stated that Gavett and Fields may have violated Sections 201 of the D.C. Firearms Control Regulation Act of 1976. That section has been codified in Section 8-1811 of the D.C. Code.

"We have reviewed the deposition transcript and agree with you that it may indicate technical violations of some of the above cited statutes. It is possible that further investigation would confirm these violations.

"However, I have decided not to ask for further investigation. Any violations which might have been committed in this context would be technical in nature and would not have been committed with a motivation that would warrant prosecution.

"Rather they would have been committed in the course of getting a weapon to and from a rifle match in North Carolina which Mr. Gavett entered as a factual redicate to bringing a lawsuit challenging the federal statute concerning the disposition of surplus firearms. . . ."

47

As a September 28, 1979 *Gun Week* article commented upon the Justice Department's cop-out, its decision "not to prosecute or even investigate a classic example of how a double standard of law exists in this country. So it must also seem to those hundreds of otherwise innocent gun owners whose lives have been ruined by fierce government prosecution of such technical and unintentional violations of the '68 Gun Control Act." In my own case, the IRS, sister agency to the Treasury Department's anti-gun Bureau of Alcohol, Tobacco and Firearms (BATF) used a technical violation on my 1978 income taxes to try ruining my life. You will never convince me that BATF had nothing to do with it.

Although Beard noted that NRA membership had fallen from a peak of one million in 1978, this temporary setback was due to an increase in NRA membership fees rather than to any undercutting of the NRA and DCM affiliation. Four years after this court decision, a bitten NRA responded by pushing its membership over the two million mark.

At the end of 1979, in response to a pro-gun film produced by the CCRKBA, "The Gun Grabbers," which was characterized as "a distorted diatribe against gun control" by NCBH, they produced "The National Handgun Awareness Test." It was a 27-minute movie which "presents the answers to the ten most important questions in the handgun control controversy . . . that is almost certain that even gun owners will at least take a moment to evaluate the reasons why such dangerous weapons are present in their homes." Actor/director Peter Bonerz narrated the film, which was also co-sponsored by the U.S. Conference of Mayors and the Foundation for Handgun Education.

The first half of 1980 was spent primarily lobbying against the enactment of the pro-gun McClure-Volkmer "Firearms Reform Act." An NCBH letter claimed that the Coalition "faces its toughest challenge since passage of the 1968 gun Control Act a dozen years ago. . . . The NRA and other no-control groups have chosen 1980 to try to dismantle the little federal gun-control legislation that exists . . . and they have already twisted enough arms to persuade 107 U.S. Congressmen to co-sponsor a disastrous new bill. . . .

"If passed (God forbid!), Senate Bill 1862 / House Bill 5225 would not merely dismantle the 1968 Gun Control Act—it would *decimate* it. . . ."

(This choice of language shows just how stupid the Gun Grabbers really are: the word *decimate* means "to reduce by one-tenth"—leaving nine-tenths intact. *Dismantle* means "to take completely apart," which to a rational person would be much worse than losing only one tenth. But *decimate* is such a flashy word NCBH hoped nobody would know what it meant. There's that "impassioned" logic at work again. Stupid, stupid.)

NCBH went on:

"But you and I *can* stop this insane return to lawlessness. . . .

"Our lobbyists are hard at work, not only to prevent passage of this new threat to the safety of all Americans, but to strengthen and support an important new gun *control* bill that is sponsored by Senator Kennedy and others."

The NCBH letter claimed "I know we will achieve everything we must," if only its members would ante-up a few more pieces of silver for the Coalition.

CURTAILMENT CAMPAIGN

In mid-year NCBH initiated a major campaign to curtail the issuance of Federal Firearms Licenses (FFLs) by the BATF. By requesting the BATF/Treasury Department to implement new regulations stipulating that FFLs would be issued or renewed only to "full time" dealers, NCBH hoped that perhaps two-thirds of the existing dealers could not re-qualify for an FFL. Thus, firearm ownership could be reduced by making it more difficult for individuals to obtain a gun when their local suppliers were forced out of business.

In a news release announcing its filing of a petition to the BATF requesting a cutback in FFLs, NCBH cried:

The BATF "is currently transmitting a dangerous message to the American people. It sounds like a matchbook cover: EARN BIG BUCKS! SELL HANDGUNS FROM YOUR HOME! DON'T WORRY ABOUT FEDERAL, STATE AND LOCAL LAWS—WE DON'T!!

"Presently ⅔ of all federal licensees are not *bona fide* businessmen and almost 80 percent are acting in violation of local, state and federal laws according to Compliance of Federal Firearms Licensees, a supportive study accompanying the petition. This study, conducted by Fields and members of the Connecticut Committee for Handgun Control, shows that 'These fraudulent and illegal federal licensees—numbering perhaps over 100,000 nationwide—are not entitled to their licenses. . . .

"The 136 holders of federal firearms dealers' licenses in the New Haven, Connecticut, metropolitan area were selected as subjects. . . . Overall, more than three-fourths (77.2 percent) of licensees were in direct violation of at lest one federal, state or local law of regulation. Nearly one-half (48.5 percent) were in violation of two or more firearms, tax or zoning require-ments."

This study later was used by the New Haven, Connecticut city council to enact an ordinance prohibiting the future is-suance or renewal of city business licenses for gun dealers within the city. However, this ordinance was later overturned by a lawsuit filed by the Second Amendment Foundation.

Following up on this study, on December 12, the NCBH and the Connecticut Committee for Handgun Control (CCHC) [a group of Connecticut and New York government officials] filed suit in Federal Court in Washington, D.C. to seek "a reform of the government's permissive licensing pro-cedures for gun dealers." The suit called on the BATF to issue dealer licenses only "to *bona fide* businessmen conducting responsible business in compliance with federal, state and local law."

Several faults were found with this request asking the BATF for implementing a new definition of gun dealer, as noted by a Jan. 30, 1981 *Gun Week* article: "thousands of FFL holders would be subjected to the arbitrary criteria of the Secretary of the Treasury as to what constitutes conducting *'bona fide'* commercial firearms activity . . . [and] in the past, many dealers who only occasionally sold firearms—such as collectors—secured FFLs solely to protect themselves from BATF's charges of 'dealing in guns without a license.' Should NCBH win in the case, these licenses may be revoked or not renewed upon expiration. The proprietors of smaller gun

businesses, and many gunsmiths, could find themselves back
to facing charges of conducting illegal 'gun dealing' because
they no longer had—nor could not get—an FFL."

As the case turned out, the court rejected *NCBH, et al. v.
BATF, et al.* and the issue was no longer of use to the Gun
Grabbers.

At year's end, NCBH was claiming 80,000 contributors and
was operating on a $450,000 budget. About a quarter of the
funds were used for congressional lobbying.

In February, 1981, Beard began hyping up his membership in a fund appeal letter by boasting:

"In our relatively short life, we've become the most serious
threat to the gun lobby's lock on the legislative process, and
to its own demented version of the American Dream: a handgun in every home (in every bed, too?).

"The National Coalition to Ban Handguns helped to pass a
tough gun control law in Washington, D.C. three years
ago. . . .

"Last year we helped New York State pass a strong law and
defeated National Rifle Association-based attempts to wipe
out the few protective provisions of the better-than-nothing
federal gun control act of 1968.

"We're helping Connecticut, Missouri, California and
Illinois draft strong gun control laws.

". . . Can you believe these pistol-packing champions of
your neighbor's right to blow your head off?. . . . The greed
and arrogance of the NRA and its fellow crazies knows no
limits."

With such respect for the dignity of others, such precision
of thought and such accuracy of statement, couldn't Michael
rake in the dough easier by hooking himself up to a steam
engine instead of writing letters? Give us a break, Michael.
I'm willing to be fair with you. I can honestly say that my
scores of debates with Michael Beard on national radio and
television shows such as the McNeil/Lehrer News Hour and
Los Angeles' NBC Sunday Show have been the best I've ever
had. Michael Beard is a sincere in-person adversary. He
doesn't hide his position. He clearly admits that he wants to
ban guns—unlike Pete Shields who cloaks his real intent
behind harmless-sounding talk and questionable statistics.

Michael Beard may get carried away with his rhetoric in print, but he runs his outfit with imagination and vigor, and he's not a snake-in-the-grass or a back stabber. You know what you're up against with Michael Beard.

MORTON GROVE

In an attempt to locate a city council which might be convinced to enact an ordinance banning the individual ownership of handguns, NCBH sent a circular proposing the scheme to numerous anti-gun groups. Upon learning that the city council of the Village of Morton Grove, Illinois was interested in the proposal, the NCBH "testified at the local hearing that led to the successful vote," and it announced that it had "agreed to pay the legal fees of the Chicago law firm" which was representing the town of 24,000 inhabitants.

"This is probably going to be the most important court test ever on the issue of the constitutionality of handgun control," Beard prophesied. An important secondary spinoff of this action was noted in an NCBH circular: "[While] the Morton Grove problem, . . . to get the federal action that is ultimately necessary, members of Congress will have to be convinced that a constituency exists—not merely the favorable majorities as measured by Gallup and Harris but a real-world constituency of voters that actively supports stronger measures. Morton Grove will help."

NATIONAL END HANDGUN VIOLENCE WEEK

In the summer of 1981, NCBH announced that it had signed up nearly 200 prominent individuals and national organizations to co-sponsor its "National End Handgun Violence Week, October 25-31st." Its purpose was:

"Raise awareness of the need for handgun control and continue to educate citizens and public officials about the tremendous costs of handgun violence. . . .

Dramatize the vast support that already exists around the country for new measures to curb handgun violence. . . .

Raise funds."

The project's chairman was the Hollywood composer and recording artist Harry Nilsson, who said: "The Coalition's National Week will involve thousands of people in the movement and will start a new, successful phase for a sane national policy on handguns."

In commemoration of this project, G.B. Trudeau, creator of the Doonesbury comic strip, drew a special poster which was distributed to colleges, churches, and community groups to publicize The Week.

"The success of National End Handgun Violence Week will be measured by the grass roots events that will take place around the country," noted Richard F. Ware, chairman of the board of NCBH. A sample of activities planned around the country included: A walk-a-thon in Chicago, "where Bill Beeck, the popular former major league baseball owner, will serve as chairman of the The Week's events, a benefit concert in Boston, a rally at UCLA, a forum at Indiana University in Bloomington, and a bike-a-thon in Waldorf, Maryland, among similar events."

Celebrities who lent their names to this event are identified in Chapter Six.

At year's end, NCBH noted that it had received donations and revenue of $773,495, but it was in the red some $44,549 as its expenses totaled $818,044. Despite NCBH's claim that it spends much of its time lobbying for anti-gun legislation, less than *one percent* of its overall expenses were spent on direct lobbying! Three percent went for "research," and only a third of one- percent was blown on "community services."

1982 wasn't expected to be as productive for NCBH as 1981. They had a little problem. After all, what can you expect for the new year when you start with revenues and donations that have fallen off by almost a *third*. NCBH found itself with only $533,671 at the beginning of 1982! The "public education" portion of their total expenses fell almost 50 percent to $234,518—but they were forced to double lobbying expenses to $20,076. Because revenues were down so drastically, total NCBH expenses had to be cut to the bone, reduced 39 percent to $502,225. All this occurred while Beard was claiming that "we've become the. most serious threat to the gun lobby's lock on the legislative process." And because of his clever tactics, to some extent he may have been right.

However, NCBH's anti-gun threat calls to mind a remark

made by British Prime Minister Winston Churchill commenting on Hitler's threat that Germany was going to wring England's chicken-little neck. While England held off repeated air attacks, Winnie retorted: "Some chicken, some neck."

HANDGUN PRODUCT LIABILITY

In late 1979 NCBH invented a novel legal theory in its efforts to curtail handgun ownership. They sought to make gun owners responsible for the criminal misuse of their handgun if stolen and then used by someone else in a crime.

On November 24, 1979, several youths broke into the National Rifle Association's office in Washington, D.C. and stole a handgun found in an NRA employee's office. Several days later, they used it for a street robbery and killed the victim. Upon reading of this incident, Sam Fields said, "There's no way God wants me to miss this opportunity." He contacted the victim's family and coaxed them into filing a multi-million dollar lawsuit against the NRA. Fields argued that the NRA had not exercised "reasonable" care in preventing a deadly weapon from falling into a criminal's hands— even though the gun belonged to an NRA employee and not the NRA.

The anti-gun strategy was that if NCBH could establish a new legal precedent that a handgun owner could be held financially liable for a criminal's misuse of a stolen gun, then millions of handgun owners would divest themselves of their weapons rather than pay several hundred dollars a year for insurance to cover themselves should one of their stolen guns be used in a crime.

NCBH won the first round. A jury on February 11, 1982 found in favor of the victim's family and against the NRA. The jury decided that the NRA had to pay more than $2 million in compensation to the victim's family. However, because the NCBH lawsuit was based on a novel legal theory, the presiding judge on July 1 overturned the jury's decision by ruling that the NRA could not be held liable for the misdeeds of a criminal.

The American Civil Liberties Union announced in early June that it was formally withdrawing as a "participating member" of the NCBH because it believes that enforcement of a handgun ban could present a threat to civil liberties. However, because it still favors more restrictive gun regulations, the ACLU said that it would become an "affiliate member."

On June 25, some 600 television, media and other celebrities paid between $25 and $100 apiece to attend the NCBH's fund-raiser dinner at the L'Enfant Plaza Hotel in Washington, D.C. Actor Elliot Gould, sporting an NCBH T-shirt, hosted the reception, along with comedians Marty Feldman and Mark Russell. When asked why he had come all the way from Los Angeles for the function, Gould replied, "I'm actively involved in disarming the world."

Another event of interest came in 1982: Common Pleas Judge Burt W. Griffin of Cleveland, Ohio, boosted NCBH's membership by one in October when he ordered postal employee Bobbie Cooper to become a life member of NCBH if he wanted to avoid being jailed for carrying a concealed pistol without a carrying permit.

According to the *Cleveland Plain Dealer*, "Griffin said he has imposed the unusual membership sentence in only about a half-dozen other cases involving carrying concealed weapons and Cooper was the only defendant to have been required to pay the lifetime fee. Griffin said Cooper could afford to pay the amount based on the salary he earned working for the Postal Service. Other defendants have paid $10 or $25 for limited membership in the organization. . . . Griffin, a strong advocate of gun control, said handguns should be banned the way switchblades, hand grenades and machine guns are. 'We cannot allow individuals to indiscriminately arm themselves,' he said."

In mid-year 1983, NCBH initiated its "THANKS Education Program" to reach both junior high and highschool students. THANKS (Teach Handgun Avoidance Now for Kids' Sake) program consists of an educational brochure explaining "the handgun menace to thousands of students across America." NCBH will also create a film to show children how to recognize a handgun, "show them the dangers of a handgun and tell them what to do if they find a handgun." Finally, the NCBH will air public-service announcements directed toward children on television stations across the country.

By early 1984, the NCBH had developed its "Political Action Committee" arm to influence congressional elections by supporting anti-gun candidates and attempting to defeat pro-gun congressmen. Judith Rossner, author of *August* and *Looking for Mr. Goodbar*, joined the NCBH-PAC's Board of Review. Upon accepting the position she said, "I'll do anything to help stop the current handgun lunacy." The NCBH claimed Rossner to be "a generous contributor to the NCBH-PAC."

Board members of the NCBH-PAC included former CIA director William Colby, authors Judith Rossner and Terry Southern, actors Teri Garr, Anne Jackson and Eli Wallach, singers Henry Nilsson and Jimmy Webb, director Peter Bonerz and Rev. Robert Drinan.

On May 25, the NCBH-PAC announced its "NOT Wanted In Congress" list of a "Dangerous Dozen" of pro-gun congressmen who it targeted for defeat in November 1984.

They were: Senators James McClure (ID) and Roger Jepsen (IA) and Representatives Harold Volkmer (MO-10), Denny Smith (OR-5), Gene Snyder (KY-4), Dan Crane (IL-19), John Kasich (OH-12), Stanford Parris (VA-8), Donald Ritter (PA-15), Michael Bilirakis (FL-9), William Carney (NY-1) and William Chappel (FL-4).

One wonders what the true criteria were that NCBH used in selecting its "hit list." This is especially so when we see that five-sixths of these nominees are Republicans and the NCBH itself went out of its way to note that Sen. McClure is a "leader in the Senate of (the) Radical Right" and he is "extremely dangerous." It would be a cheap shot to note that Sen. McClure isn't as dangerous as the Hero of Chappaquiddick, Gun Grabber Sen. Edward Kennedy—nobody's died in McClure's car—so I won't say it.

In announcing its "hit list," NCBH Chairman Michael Beard said, "Because we have limited financial resources, we will target our efforts on The Dangerous Dozen, twelve men in Congress who . . . have consistently opposed sensible handgun control laws . . . and who have taken thousands of dollars in campaign funds from the National Rifle Association. . . . As a group, the Dangerous Dozen has received nearly $100,000 from the NRA.

"Most of the Dangerous Dozen . . . won their last election by a narrow margin. A shift in a small number of votes could make a crucial difference. This year, we are going to be asking voters in selected congressional districts and states to vote as if their lives depended on it.

". . . Another priority is to send a message to every member of Congress who takes campaign money from the gun lobby and sponsors the McClure-Volkmer bill, a message that says that the majority of Americans will no longer tolerate a legislative process that is warped and distorted because of the narrow, selfish interests of the gun lobby."

Beard, who, incidentally, is a former Ted Kennedy staff member, evidently wants to create a legislative process that is warped and distorted because of the narrow, selfish interests of the anti-gun lobby. Unfortunately for gun owners, he's good at it.

3

The Gun Grabber Network

As we saw in our first chapters, the two "Gun Grabber Biggies," HCI and NCBH, are bad news for gun owners. But now we have to face the rest of the trouble: behind the "Biggies" stands an elaborate network of anti-gun agitators throughout the United States. Some of these "networked" groups are sizeable multi-purpose organizations with their own gun control department or committee, such as the United States Conference of Mayors; some are established institutions with an interest in gun issues, such as religious bodies; and some are smaller single purpose Gun Grabber groups that we'll investigate in detail. Together they form the "Gun Grabbers Network." Gun owner, if you think the "Network" can be dismissed, read on!

Citizen "networks" usually have two different kinds of component groups: those that know about each other and deliberately work together, and those that work on the issue but have little actual contact with each other and are part of the network out of a "conspiracy of shared values" more than any formal connections. The Gun Grabbers Network consists of both types of group. Their network extends all across the country; it is geographically and demographically diverse. And it works like hell to yank all guns out of your hands.

THE HEARTLAND

To get some idea of what the 'Network' is up to, let's examine it group by group and place by place, beginning in America's Midwestern heartland, Illinois. One of the more fascinating parts of the Network is the Illinois Citizens for Handgun Control (ICHC) and their affiliate, the Committee for the Study of Handgun Misuse (CFSHM)—both use the

59

same address: 109 N. Dearborn, Suite 704, Chicago, IL 60602. Again, I know that all these abbreviations such as ICHC and CFSHM sound like alphabet soup, but in print there's really no other way to deal with outfits that have such cumbersome names, so grit your teeth and bear with me some more.

ICHC adopted its present name in the Spring of 1982: it had originally organized in September 1973 as the Committee for Handgun Control (CFHC). Even before the name change, ICHC was a lobbying group as it is today, trying to influence both city councils and state legislative hearings. It developed the CFSHM as a tax-deductible affiliate.

This tax-deductible affiliate, according to its materials, seeks to "bring to the attention of citizens the threat that the continued indiscriminate sale and use of handguns impose on society. We are working for strong enforceable federal legislation to control handguns—to effectively eliminate their use except for law enforcement and sporting use."

CFSHM studies cases and compiles data on handgun misuse throughout the United States. In 1981, it was designated a national resource center on this issue by the U.S. Conference of Mayors Handgun Control Project. In order to "inform" the public, CFSHM publishes fact sheets, brochures, pamphlets and other materials.

It helped coordinate the October 31, 1981 "Run Against the Handgun" marathon in Morton Grove, Illinois. Chicago Cub Ernie Banks ran in the 10- kilometer event.

The CFSHM developed an "Education Curriculum on Handgun Violence" for use by school teachers. It is a three-part two-hour module whereby, "First, students filled out an attitude questionnaire on handguns and then discussed their responses. Teachers followed this activity with a 'Handgun Squares' game based on the popular television program [Hollywood Squares]. The questions and answers concerned facts about handguns and handgun laws. Finally, the students were given scripts and then enacted situations which could lead to handgun violence."

The CFSHM is quite candid about the intent of its school anti-handgun "brainwash" program: "We're trying to present a curriculum so that students can think about their own feelings and examine the consequences of handgun misuse, as well as learn some of the facts about handguns. We also hope that we can *counteract* the glamour and status that the media and culture place on handguns."

CFSHM has a number of such "educational" committees for helping to spread its gospel. They include: a Speakers Bureau, a Victims Family Committee, the Medical Council on Handgun Violence, an Educational Committee, and a Conference and Seminar Committee.

Individuals associated with this group either today or in the past include: Estelle Jacobson (ex-president), Katherine Zartman (president), Derry Henderson (vice-president), and Kathryn Rowe (speakers bureau). Past directors: Susan Sullivan, Sally Campbell, Florence McMillan, Valerie True, Martha McNeill, Ginny Christenson, Kitty North, Georgene Campion, Cilia Molony, and Lynn Moor.

Now, this arm called the Medical Council on Handgun Violence (MCHV) mentioned above is a stroke of Gun Grabber genius: it arouses both respect and emotion at the same time. It uses the basic CFSHV address, c/o Committee for the Study of Handgun Violence, 109 N. Dearborn, Suite 701, Chicago, IL 60602. MCHV was founded in 1980 and according to its literature believes, "that the alarming rise in handgun violence must be viewed as a public health problem. By keeping concerned health care professionals informed about the problem of handgun violence, the Medical Council helps prepare them for their most important objective—the educating of the public about the disease itself."

Founding members of the Medical Council on Handgun Violence include:

Whitney Addington, M.D. Head, Pulmonary Section, The University of Chicago;

Robert Baker, M.D., Professor of Surgery, The University of Illinois at the Medical Center, Chicago, IL;

John Beal, M.D., Chairman, Northwestern University Medical School;

Henry Betts, M.D., Medical Director of The Rehabilitation Institute of Chicago;

Leonard Cerullo, M.D., Assistant Professor of Surgery, Northwestern University Medical School;

Edmund Donoghue, Jr., M.D., Deputy Chief Medical Examiner, Officer of the Medical Examiner, Cook County, IL;

Norton Flanagan, M.D., The Rehabilitation Institute of Chicago;

Robert Freeark, M.D., Chairman, Department of Surgery, Loyola University Medical Center, Maywood, IL;

Professor Willard Fry, M.D., Northwestern University Medical School;

James Hines, M.D., Chief, Section of General Surgery, Northwestern University Medical School;

Olga Jonasson, M.D., Chief of Surgery, Cook County Hospital;

David McLone, M.D. Chairman of Pediatric Neurosurgery, Children's Memorial Hospital;

Lawrence Michaelis, M.D., Northwestern University Medical School;

Professor Vincent O'Conor, Jr., M.D. Northwestern University Medical School;

Professor Clyde Phillips, M.D. University. of Illinois at the Medical Center, Chicago, IL;

Professor Anthony Raimondi, M.D., Northwestern University Medical School;

Professor Robert Replogle, M.D., University of Chicago;

Vinod Sahgal, M.D. The Rehabilitation Institute of Chicago;

Robert Stein, M.D., Cook County Chief Medical Examiner;

Alex Tulsky, M.D. Michael Reese Hospital; and

Associate Professor David Turner, M.D., Rush Medical College.

The agreement of medical professionals to act as catspaws for a "social engineering" project by the Gun Grabbers verges on an outright breach of professional ethics. For the Gun Grabbers of CFSHM to assert that handgun violence is "a disease" is tantamount to practicing medicine without a license.

At least the story of the Illinois Handgun Control Association has a happy ending, thanks to—of all people—notorious anti-gun syndicated columnist Mike Royko. On June 20, 1982, in the *Chicago Sun-Times* Royko headlined a column, "Phony Shot Down." Royko raised the question of whether IHCA leader Larry Dolan was doing anything to control handguns, rather than just soliciting funds for the alleged purpose of planning to do so. A few days after Royko's column appeared, Dolan announced that he was closing down the IHCA—due to bad publicity.

You saw the name Katherine Zartman in the list of CFSHM officers above, remember? Well, this busy lady is also a past president of the precursor outfit known as the Chicago Committee for Handgun Control (CCHC), PO Box 207, Kenilworth, IL 60043. Take it from me, she is not afraid to speak out against guns. I have seen her at first hand when I debated her on Chicago television. On February 12, 1980, CCHC held its first annual Lincoln Day Dinner in support of "Handgun Awareness Day." Mayor Richard Hatcher of Gary, Indiana, received the CCHC's first Lincoln Day Award, which was a "handgun fashioned into the form of a scorpion," for his "untiring efforts to address handgun abuse in his city." A keynote address was given by Sheriff John J. Buckley of Massachusetts, about whom more later.

Another Chicago Gun Grabber Network group, although somewhat intermittent in its operations, is the Civic Disarmament Committee for Handgun Control (CDC), 5532 South Shore Drive, Chicago, IL 60637. A woman named Lauri Fermi, wife of the famous nuclear physicist Enrico Fermi, was chairman of CDC, a citizens group in support of the ban on the manufacture, sale, interstate transportation, and private possession of handguns. As a nuclear engineer myself I have long admired Dr. Fermi's work. But Mrs. Fermi is another matter. As a debating partner on a Chicago TV station, I thought she was inarticulate, an embarrassment to the anti-gun movement. I felt sorry for her. Her group, CDC, stressed public education and supported both state and federal legislation.

Its frequent off-and-on-again activities support various state and local ordinances tightening up on the sale and ownership of handguns.

Past addresses have been: 111 E. Wacker Drive, Chicago, IL 60601; 5801 Dorchester Ave., Chicago, IL 60637

As we leave the Illinois branch of the Gun Grabber Network, we have to mention that apple-pie-and-motherhood organization, the national Parent-Teachers Association (PTA), headquartered in Chicago. Why? Well, delegates to the 79th national convention of the PTA voted to support the following statements:

"The National PTA supports legislation that will restrict the manufacture of handguns and handgun ammunition, and

"That the PTA supports legislation which will ban the manufacture, importation, assembly or sale of the 'Saturday Night Special.' "

THE WEST COAST

And now, out to the West Coast to California, which has been described by agriculturally conscious wags as the "land of fruits and nuts." Here the Gun Grabber Network can boast of the Committee for Handgun Control (CHC), 8455 Beverly Boulevard, Los Angeles, CA 90048. Founded in 1973, "The Committee" is a statewide group whose aim is to support effective handgun control legislation and to promote an awareness of "the dangers of the indiscriminate availability and usage of handguns." Early in the 1980s the CHCH appealed to the U.S. Consumer Product Safety Commission to declare that bullets are a hazardous substance, but its effort failed. The Committee supported California's 1982 Proposition 15 "handgun freeze" referendum. Dee Helfgott and Elle Jacobson used to work for CHC.

There was also a Southern California Committee for Handgun Control, PO Box 2231, Van Nuys, CA 94117. A Joy Dell was president in 1977, but little has been heard from this group lately.

On the other hand, the Northern California Coalition for Handgun Control, 501 Masonic, San Francisco, CA 94117, was busy in 1977 and still kicks up a fuss now and then. In early 1977 they convinced the San Francisco Board of Permit Appeals to deny four gun retailers permits to sell handguns. In December 1983, the board had voted to disapprove all future permits for the sale of concealable weapons in an effort to reduce street crime.

Up in the Pacific Northwest, the Washington Citizens for Rational Handgun Controls is a Gun Grabbers Network group based in Seattle, Washington. Steve Kendall and Karl Forsgaard are two names associated with this group, which has lobbied various Washington communities to tighten up their controls over firearm sales. Steve Kendall and I have sparred on a number of occasions on radio and television as well as on college campuses in the Northwest.

Off the mainland in Hawaii, the Schutter Foundation of Honolulu is the network affiliate. Founded in 1981 by Honolulu attorney David Schutter to "educate the public about the necessity of banning handguns in Hawaii." At its inception, the following individuals served on the foundation's board: attorney Wallace Fujiyama; Muliufi Hannemann, special assistant to Governor Ariyoshi; Professor Gregory Yee Mark; Ah Quon McElrath, administrative assistant of ILWU Local 142; Tom Naki; Marc Oley; Julianne Puzon, a researcher in Lieutenant Governor King's office; and the Reverend Jory Watland, pastor of Christ the King Lutheran Church in Kalihi. Mike Keller was appointed executive director.

MID-AMERICA AGAIN

Back in middle America, down below the Mason-Dixon line, we find the National Alliance of Handgun Control Education (NAHCE), formerly the National Alliance of Handgun Control Organizations, PO Box 40451, Nashville, Tennessee, 37204. This outfit is probably the most "networked" group of the Gun Grabbers Network. It had a peculiar beginning. Go back to the U.S. Conference of Mayors' "National Conference on Handgun Violence" in November 1979. There, representatives of state and local handgun control organizations, citing the need for increased cooperation and information sharing, voted unanimously to form the "National Alliance of Handgun Control Organizations." In mid-1983 its name underwent a slight change, dropping "Organizations" in favor of "Education."

In the past the following individuals have served as elected NAHCE officers: Katherine Zartman, president, who is also affiliated with the Illinois Citizens for Handgun Control; Don Hesse, vice-president, of California; Louis Schaul, treasurer, of Cleveland; Derry Henderson, secretary, of Cleveland; Donald Maillie (past president) of Nashville; Estelle Jacobson (past vice-president) of the Chicago Committee for Handgun Control; and Anita Griedman (past secretary-treasurer) of the Gun Control Federation of Greater Cleveland.

NAHCO held its first Annual Meeting in Chicago on May 8 through 10, 1980. Mayor Jayne Byrne proclaimed May 8 as "Handgun Control Day," and talk-show host Phil Donahue at a rally at the Daly Civic Center Plaza said, "Handgun control will not eliminate all murders; it will not eliminate anti- social behavior; but it will reduce the number of innocent victims." Other attendees included actress Mrs. (Marlo Thomas) Phil Donahue, John Anderson (former U.S. Representative and part-time presidential candidate), and actress Cloris Leachman. Speaking of Phil Donahue, his TV show is one of the few national shows that has refused to allow me to appear. My publicity director was told by a Donahue Show staffer that Phil doesn't want to debate gun control with someone like me who knows the issue better than he does and who works on it on a daily basis. So much for the strength of his convictions.

Tennessee also appears to be the home of Tennesseeans for Handgun Control, Inc., PO Box 40451, Nashville, TN 37204, but the only lasting contribution to the Gun Grabber cause this group seems to have made is loaning its president, Don Maillie, to NAHCE for a stint as their president.

Just as "Tennesseeans for Handgun Control, Inc." appears to be a miscellaneous Gun Grabber Network group, so numerous anti-gun organizations throughout the country seem to work in isolation or simply contribute people to other groups from time to time. Here's a smattering to give you some idea how large the whole menagerie is:

Georgians for Handgun Control, Inc.
PO Box 8273
Atlanta, GA 30306

Maryland Committee for Handgun Control
PO Box 4526
Baltimore, MD 21212

Homicide Reduction Through Education
1817 Stanhope
Grosse Pointe Woods, MI 48236

Citizens United to Save Lives
Chairman Dwite Walker; Vice-Chairman Reverend Gary
Wheeler;
Secretary Mrs. Roberta Adler; Treasurer Terry Murphy
Box 5038
Grosse Point Station, MI 48236

CUSL "wholly believes a total ban is the answer to the
handgun problem." This citizen group is locally based, but
has allegedly thousands of members throughout the state.
Dwite Walker, chairman, directs CUSL in its support of local
and federal legislation and in "educating the public to the
need for gun control."

Detroit Handgun Crisis Task Force
(Project of the Detroit Urban League)
Frank Kornegay, executive director
Albert J. Dunmore, president
208 Mack Avenue
Detroit, MI 48201

Missouri Committee for Firearms Safety
Eugene Schwartz
7202 Pershing
University City, MO 63130

Council for a Responsible Firearms Policy, Inc.
James B. Sullivan, director
826 First Street S.E.
Minot, North Dakota 58701

Criminal Justice Public Information Center
3510 Chester Avenue
Cleveland, OH 44114

Handgun Control Federation of Ohio
435 Leader Building
Cleveland, OH 44114
(216)-541-9225

Gun Control Federation of Greater Cleveland
Joseph B. Clough, past president
1315 Terminal Tower
Cleveland, OH 44113

Pennsylvania Coalition to Control Handguns
Ms. Alice Herzon
1700 Walnut St., Suite 1004
Philadelphia, PA 19103

Handgun Alert, Inc.
Mrs. Charles Potter, past president
PO Box 6771
Providence, RI 02904

It is interesting that on my national media tours television and radio shows have a hard time getting representatives to appear against me from local "Gun Grabber Network" groups. They seem to prefer to go unchallenged with their attacks on the rights of gun owners.

TEXAS

We can't leave the middle tier of states without a stopover in the great state of Texas, the Lone Star State. Most Texans are less fond of Gun Grabbers than they are of scorpions and rattlesnakes, but one son of the Texas soil seems to love them. His name is Windle Turley. He's the president of Windle Turley, P.C., Attorneys and Counselors, a Dallas law firm that has gone to bat for the Gun Grabbers trying to stretch liability law to the breaking point.

Turley is batting zero so far, but he hopes that firing off a barrage of lawsuits aimed at making handgun manufacturers liable for the damage inflicted by their weapons will eventually hit a home run for the Gun Grabbers. The 45-year-old Turley has filed dozens of suits and lost all that have come to trial as of this writing. But it would only take one win to virtually ban handguns in America.

Turley's ammunition is strict-liability law, a 22-year-old theory that claims the manufacturer is responsible for un- reasonable dangers caused by a product. The cause of action in these lawsuits is not conventional negligence. It is "pro- ducts liability" under "strict liability," which holds that "a manufacturer is strictly liable in tort when an article he places in the market, knowing that it is to be used without inspection for defects, proves to have a defect that causes injury to a human being." In the 1970s lawyers began to successfully assert such claims against products ranging from drugs and pesticides to non-fire-retardant children's sleepwear. A hand- gun, Turley argues, is inherently and exclusively a "tool of destruction" that "when marketed to the general public, poses an unacceptable risk of injury and harm to society."

Who is this knot in the Gun Grabber net? If you looked at his law firm's glossy, glitzy magazine-size brochure, you'd think from the over-glorious cover illustration that Windle Turley was Perry Mason, Sherlock Holmes and Ralph Nader rolled into one. Then if you read the self-important descrip- tion of Turley's law firm, you'd think someone had added Horatio Alger, The Lone Ranger and P.T. Barnum into the package. Here's how they describe themselves:

"From 1973 when Windle Turley started this firm with one secretary, until today, where sixteen attorneys, with a sup- port staff of more than seventy-five now practice, two things have not changed: the firm's *Commitment To Quality Service and A Winning Tradition.*

"Recognizing the common law as a living and growing insti- tution that can, through change, diminish human suffering and injustice, the firm has created a *Stimulating Professional Environment*, that compels it *beyond* the traditional trial firm.

"With a practice and reputation already national in scope, it proudly enters its second exciting decade. We are confident the aggressive and bright trial lawyers assembled in this firm, supported by the most modern litigation methods and com- municating technology, will enable us to fully and success- fully serve our clients.

"Whether the cause be a slight injury wrongfully imposed, or an unnecessary human death, we remain dedicated to full justice for our clients and the *Elimination of the Cause* of unnecessary human suffering."

You can hear the violins in the background. His writers almost sound like refugees from Superman comics. But Windle Turley is no joke. A graduate of Southern Methodist University Law School (1965), he has received wide publicity as the subject of a CBS News *60 Minutes* profile and a *Newsweek* feature among other media coverage. He is publicly on record as having set aside a quarter of a million dollars to pursue the cases of dozens of handgun "victims" he has taken on as clients. And his firm's "Research and Development programs" are bad news for gun owners.

As the Turley firm's brochure tells us, "Many theories and procedures that are now routine in this firm had their genesis as in-house R & D Programs. Among them: successful efforts, beginning in 1972, to make aircraft and tractor-truck manufacturers liable for *Non-Crashworthy Designs*; and the development in 1979 of the *Video Documentary* as a settlement tool in plaintiffs' cases.

"Current R & D projects include: Development of *Video Trials, Computerized Case Management Programs* and *Tort Remedies for Handgun Victims*. The latter two R & D programs have full-time staffs and are multi-year endeavors.

"Perhaps the most far-reaching and ambitious project yet undertaken by the firm is its program to develop tort remedies for the victims of this country's annual 22,000 deaths and 200,000 handgun injuries, almost none of whom have reasonable legal remedies today. The attorneys and staff assigned to this 3 year project are confident the suits in more than a dozen states will stimulate recoveries for handgun victims and a modified view of the suppliers' responsibility for handgun violence."

These efforts to lay the blame for handgun crime at the factory gate are serious indeed. Fortunately for gun owners, courts are not buying Turley's arguments—so far. Turley's first manufacturer liability case came to trial and was decided against him on January 20, 1984, in Dallas, Texas. A four-man, eight-woman jury deliberated for nearly ten hours over whether David Duane Clancy should be awarded damages from Arms Corporation of America and Zale Corporation, who made and sold the gun used to paralyze Clancy in a schoolyard shooting in 1977. According to testimony, Clancy, then 15, was paralyzed from the shoulders down when a .22-caliber revolver in the hands of classmate Kenneth Hacker was discharged and fired a bullet into Clancy's neck, where it remains. Hacker testified he had bought the gun two weeks earlier from another student for $10 and was showing it to a girl in his car when it went off, hitting Clancy who was standing nearby.

The jury decided that Clancy should be awarded $2 million in damages, but that any damages should be paid by Hacker, who was holding the gun when it fired. Hacker, of course, is unlikely to ever be able to pay even a tiny fraction of this award. The jury specifically and unequivocally rejected Turley's unorthodox contention that the firms which manufactured and sold the gun be held liable for over $43 million in damages.

While the Clancy case shot down Turley's product liability theory in a jury trial, it did not clearly spell out the legal reasoning and precedents which are so important to a society based on law and order. On August 28, 1984, Chief Judge Tom Stagg of the United States District Court, Western District of Louisiana, Shreveport Division, solved that deficiency. He dismissed all claims of plaintiff policeman Marion Eugene Watson, his wife Nelwyn and their four children, against Brauer Brothers Manufacturing Company, makers of a gun holster that was the center of another Windle Turley lawsuit.

In this case, Watson and family had asked $5 million in two lawsuits. The first suit asked to recover damages for injuries sustained as a result of his use of an alleged defectively designed pistol holster issued to him by his employer, the Shreveport Police Department. In the second suit Watson's wife and children sought damages under Louisiana law for "loss of consortium." The suits were combined for the two-day bench trial (no jury) in Shreveport which began August 16, 1984.

While on routine patrol checking out a convenience store

on March 2, 1982, Watson had been shot several times with his own gun by assailant Robert Pettaway. Pettaway had removed Watson's gun from its holster when brushing against the officer while passing him in a store aisle. Neither Watson nor the store clerk was immediately aware that the officer's revolver had been removed. Pettaway was later convicted of the shooting and imprisoned.

Watson's case was based upon the allegation that his "border patrol" style holster, manufactured by another but sold by Brauer Brothers under its own imprint, was defectively designed. Since the assailant had so easily removed the service revolver, Watson's attorneys claimed the holster was "unreasonably dangerous for normal use." They also claimed that the manufacturer "failed to warn of the dangers inherent in the product." The case then turned on the product's main safety feature, its safety strap, and whether or not Watson had properly snapped it.

Watson testified that he had entered the convenience store with his holster's safety strap properly snapped over his weapon. Dr. Kevin Parsons, an expert called by Watson's attorneys, testified that the border patrol safety strap is one of the least effective means of weapons retention because the strap is on the outside, more accessible to a possible assailant. The "thumb break" strap and snap is better, Parsons said, because it is located on the inside (belt side) of the holster. The "sight track" feature is also better, Parsons said, because the gun sight must travel out of the holster on a track at a certain angle to pull freely—if someone pulls from the wrong angle, the sight will catch because the track is not followed.

Brauer Brothers then had their expert testify, Mr. John Cayton, a crime scene reconstruction specialist. Cayton demonstrated in the courtroom how an assailant can remove a gun from a holster—using Brauer Brothers' attorney as a model wearing the gear. Cayton showed that a gun in a border patrol holster with a properly snapped safety strap could not be removed, period. Just to be sure, Judge Stagg took the gear, experts and attorneys into his chambers and tried to remove the gun himself. He later wrote: "The weapon could not be removed. The strap did *not* release."

Brauer Brothers attorneys also introduced evidence that

recently developed weapon retention courses such as those by James Lindell, considered the foremost authority, are a vital and now mandatory part of officer safety training. Lindell teaches that no holster currently available is foolproof and that other training is necessary in retaining weapons. Watson entered the Shreveport force in 1969, and their Academy's weapon retention program did not begin until 1981. Although Watson could have taken the training as an in- service officer, he testified that he could not remember being instructed in such programs.

With the facts before him, Judge Stagg then addressed the questions of law. A "threshold question" arose: is Brauer Brothers liable under Louisiana law since they did not actually produce the holster in this case? A manufacturer which holds a product out as its own *is* liable as the actual manufacturer, *LeBouef v. Goodyear Tire & Rubber Company*, 623 F.2d 985 (5th Cir. 1980).

Under Louisiana law, Stagg noted, a manufacturer of a product is liable for injury sustained because of "a defect in the design or manufacture of the article, if the injury might reasonably have been anticipated." A plaintiff claiming damages, however, has the burden of proof that the product was "defective, unreasonably dangerous to normal use, and that the plaintiff's injuries were caused by reason of the defect," *Weber v. Fidelity & Casualty Insurance Company of New York*, 259 La. 559, 250 So.2d 754 (La. 1971).

If the product is proven defective by reasons of hazards to normal use, the plaintiff need not prove actual negligence by the maker, *Weber, supra*. "Normal use" is slippery, however. The law does not require the manufacturer make the product "fool proof" or "accident proof." *But . . .*

The law requires reasonable care to design products to prevent "foreseeable injuries" in "reasonably expected" uses. A manufacturer can also be held liable if injury results from lack of adequate warning that renders the product unreasonably dangerous, *Chappius v. Sears, Roebuck & Co.*, 358 So.2d 926 (La. 1978). But, "where the danger and manner of avoiding that danger are matters of common knowledge, the manufacturer has no duty to warn," *Guidry v. Kem Manufacturing Co.* 693 F.2d 426 (5th Cir. 1982).

The final arguments?Brauer Brothers contended that Watson assumed the risk of injury. Judge Stagg noted the Louisiana Supreme Court recently explained the doctrine: "It is fundamental that in order to assume a risk, one must knowingly and voluntarily encounter a risk which caused him harm." On the other hand, Watson contended that the holster 1) was unreasonably dangerous for police officers, and 2) the manufacturer should have issued an appropriate warning.

Judge Stagg ruled that the trial evidence leads to the inescapable conclusion that the Brauer Brothers holster was not "unreasonably dangerous for normal use." A reasonable seller, knowing the risk of "foreseeable injuries" if the gun could be removed by an assailant with the strap unsnapped would still offer this holster for sale. No holster was shown safer. It is "common knowledge" that border patrol holster straps are safer when snapped than unsnapped, so there was "no duty to warn."

Since neither Watson nor the store clerk indicated that a struggle ensued when Pettaway removed the officer's weapon, and Watson's holster showed no damage, normally evident when a gun is forcibly removed, Judge Stagg ruled that Watson's safety strap *had not been snapped* during the incident. Since Watson knew the dangers of unsnapped safety straps, Stagg ruled Watson's actions constituted "a voluntary choice to encounter a known risk."

Therefore, Watson and his attorneys failed to meet their burden of proof in establishing that Officer Watson's injuries were in any way chargeable to the fault of Brauer Brothers. Judge Stagg dismissed all claims against the defendant. That's the great holster case. Thank you, Judge Stagg, for an elegant piece of legal reasoning that defenders of the Second Amendment will admire for ages to come. Take that, Windle Turley!

Judge Stagg must be smiling, because his reasoning was upheld on June 17, 1985, by the Fifth Circuit U.S. Court of Appeals in New Orleans, the highest court that has yet heard a case involving the Windle Turley theory. The appeals court that day rejected a suit brought by Turley that had been combined by the court with another similar suit, the cases of

Perkins v. FIE (a firearms manufacturer) and Richman v. Charter Arms (Turley's case).

Earlier District Court Judge Henry Mentz had denied Charter Arms' motion for a dismissal. In fact, in a long 30-page opinion, Judge Mentz had written that the selling of guns was an "ultrahazardous activity." Pat Squire, attorney for FIE, said, "That was a new twist to the defectless product liability theory." Charter Arms appealed. A few weeks before that a federal judge had granted FIE's motion for dismissal, saying there was no cause for action. When the plaintiffs appealed, the court combined the FIE case with the Charter Arms suit.

"These were opposite decisions on the exact same point of law in the same federal circuit," said Squire. In the Perkins case, Joseph Perkins had sued FIE, claiming he was shot by a .25-caliber pistol they had manufactured. In the Richman case, Judie Richman claimed her daughter was shot and killed with a .38-caliber handgun made by Charter Arms. Turley brought the Richman suit.

But the Fifth Circuit Court of Appeals would have none of the product liability arguments of the Texas lawyer. The court ruled, "The marketing of handguns to the general public falls far beyond the boundaries of the Louisiana doctrine of ultra-hazardous activity. The injuries of which the plaintiffs complain were not caused by the marketing itself, but rather resulted only when there was substandard conduct on the part of third parties."

A ruling that the marketing of handguns constitutes an ultrahazardous activity "would in practice drive manufacturers out of business" and "would produce a handgun ban by judicial fiat."

The court noted the Louisiana Supreme Court had defined "unreasonably dangerous" to mean "simply that the article which injured the plaintiff was dangerous to an extent beyond that which would be contemplated by an ordinary consumer." The three judges concluded that "whether an activity should be classified as 'ultrahazardous' is a question of law, and we hold that the plaintiffs in this case cannot recover under that theory. And because the guns functioned precisely as they were designed, and because the dangers of handguns are obvious and well-known to all members of the consuming public, we hold that the plaintiffs cannot recover, as a matter of law, under Louisiana products liability law, either under the consumers expectations test . . . or under the risk/utility test."

Even though this is the highest court to sack Windle Turley so far, this decision is probably not the one that stung him most. That would undoubtedly have to be the 1985 case of Patterson v. Rohm, heard by U.S. District Court Judge Jerry Buchmeyer in Dallas, Texas. Buchmeyer is a rip- snorting anti-gun judge and Windle Turley couldn't even get a favorable ruling on his weird products liability theory from Buchmeyer. Buchmeyer wrote, "As an individual, I believe very strongly that handguns should be banned. . . . However, as a judge I know full well that the question of whether they can be sold is a political one, not an issue of products liability law—and that is a matter for the legislatures, not the courts."

Buchmeyer dismissed a suit filed by a woman whose son, James Patterson, was shot and killed with a Rohm .38-caliber revolver by a would-be robber at a Dallas 7-Eleven store where Patterson was a clerk. Turley, the attorney for Jett Edwards Patterson, claimed that the woman deserved $500,000 in damages from Rohm Gesellschaft, the West German gun manufacturer, because the risks of injury and death from handguns "greatly outweigh any utility they may have, which makes the guns unreasonably dangerous."

Turley and his associates "simply want to eliminate handguns," Buchmeyer wrote. The judge noted that most legislators, "certainly those in Texas—do not consider that the manufacture and sale of handguns to the public is unreasonably dangerous or is socially unacceptable." He pointed out that in 1981 alone the Texas Legislature defeated 18 gun-control bills.

Linda Turley, who handles many of the handgun product liability cases for the Turley firm, told the *Dallas Times Herald* she was not pleased with the outcome of the suit, "but it's not so disappointing that we're ready to give up these kinds of cases."

But don't think we've heard the last of this aggressive Gun Grabber, fellow citizens. As this book went to press, the record showed that Turley had filed more than 80 product liability suits against handguns.

As a miscellaneous note while we're in the Southern tier of states, Florida spawned a rash of anti-gun groups supporting the March 1984 vote giving Broward County power to enact countywide handgun regulations, including the Handgun Control Network of Palm Beach County and the Florida Coalition to Halt Handgun Crime, a Miami group.

THE EAST COAST

Now let's take a leisurely stroll down the East Coast, that bastion of tradition and history. In Massachusetts we find the Crime and Justice Foundation, 100 Franklin Street or 31 St. James Ave., Suite 348, Boston, MA 02110. This Gun Grabber Network group with the odd-sounding name claims a long past: "The Crime and Justice Foundation is a hundred year old multipurpose criminal justice education organization (formerly the Massachusetts Council on Crime and Delinquency that published the handbook *Shooting Gallery Called America*) which supports strict handgun control." John D. Carver was once its deputy director.

Up the road a bit we find another group with an odd-sounding name, People vs. Handguns, Box 229, Newton, Massachusetts 02160. PVH is a non-profit citizens group dedicated to handgun control in Massachusetts. PVH initiated a statewide referendum in 1976 to ban handguns, but the voters rejected the measure. PVH also provides speakers for debates and educational materials.

The origin of PVH was described in a mild-mannered U.S. Conference of Mayors handbook, *People Vs. Handguns: The Campaign To Ban Handguns in Massachusetts*: "If it had not been for the insulting and loud demeanor of the sportsmen at the 1973 Public Safety Committee hearings the initiative petition to ban handguns may never have come to fruition." Following that meeting, Sheriff Buckley's press advisor Peter Nichols approached the sheriff with the concept about their filing an initiative to put the handgun-ban measure on the ballot—Buckley favored the challenge.

Because of the projected high expenses for their initiative, Nichols suggested that a non-profit (but not tax deductible) organization be established to spearhead the petition campaign; thus this Massachusetts anti-handgun Frankenstein was conceived. Because PVH was involved in a political campaign, contributions were not tax-deductible.

According to the U.S. Conference of Mayors report, "Early support for People vs. Handguns came from the Massachusetts Council of Churches, the Paulist Center of Boston, and the Bishop of the Massachusetts Episcopal Archdiocese, John M. Burgess. Also the Massachusetts State Federation of Womens Clubs, long an advocate of handgun control on the national level, readily offered its endorsement." Later the Massachusetts League of Women Voters decided that it "believes private citizens should not have access to handguns."

To encourage people to sign the petition, Boston Red Sox pitcher Bill Lee visited several supermarkets in Quincy urging shoppers to sign the PVF petition. In one case, "a man entering the market signed the petition in exchange for Bill Lee's autograph."

At one time or another the following individuals have been associated with PVH: Sheriff John Buckley of Middlesex County served as president after founding the group in March 1974; Judy Holmberg was executive director; Diane Litsis, director; Janet Wohlberg, vice president; and Stephen Stone, treasurer. (Stone is president of Converse Rubber Company.) I have debated Sheriff Buckley on the David Brudnoy Show on WRKO radio in Boston. Banning your guns is the number one goal in his life.

Despite the rejection of its ideas by Massachusetts voters in 1976, PVF continues today to lobby the state legislature to enact ever-tougher statewide gun controls.

In the next state south, the Connecticut Committee for Handgun Control, Steve Masters, president, is the Gun Grabbers Network affiliate. CCHC convinced the city council of New Haven in December 1979 to ban the sale of handguns within the city limits. However, a Second Amendment Foundation lawsuit overturned the ban in court.

As usual, the real dillies are in New York. Ah, inimitable New York. Here in the Big Apple we can't avoid the National Alliance Against Violence (NAAV), (formerly the Foundation on Violence in America (FVA). In mid-1982, *Rolling Stone* publisher Jann Wenner announced the formation of FVA (NAAV) as a novel weapon to advance the cause of gun control. He decided that by locating anti-gun policemen, and after refining their speaking skills, he could then make fund-raising speaking engagements for them around the country to attack civilian ownership of handguns.

Jenner's tactics drew their inspiration from a poll he conducted a year earlier which showed that Americans consider their local police chief the most credible source of information about handguns.

Jenner's involvement in the Gun Grabber Crusade was spurred by the shooting death of his friend John Lennon.

A *Washington Post* article described Jenner's beliefs: "The most sensible strategy is for gun control advocates to stay away from legislative fights for a period of time and focus instead on a long-term public education campaign in which they seize the high ground of moderation, reasonableness and common sense."

NAAV's board members include: *Readers Digest* editor-in-chief Edward Thompson, former Secretary of State Cyrus Vance, ex-Representative Paul McCloskey, former Urban League leader Vernon Jordan, and Chicago Police Superintendent Richard J. Brzeczek. That may explain why *Readers Digest* has refused to run paid advertisements from the Second Amendment Foundation.

One of NAAV's first projects, according to NAAV executive director Betsy Gotbaum, was to convince the police departments of Chicago, New York City, Minneapolis, and Fresno and Fremont, California, to provide spokesmen who would tour their communities and urge their residents not to possess handguns. Referring to California's Proposition 15 "handgun freeze" referendum, Gotbaum said: "It's the bellwether for the country. If California passes that legislation it's going to be extremely meaningful." As a matter of fact, the voters rejected the freeze by a two-to-one margin in November, 1982, but somehow the Gun Grabbers didn't think that was "extremely meaningful."

According to IRS documents, NAAV spent nearly $80,000 during 1982. $23,405 went for a poll studying the public's attitudes about firearms; $55,293 was shot to develop a project "to mobilize and activate police efforts to reduce handgun violence at a community level;" and $32,000 was used to pay salaries and wages for NAAV staffers. NAAV received $166,445 in contribution, and after expenses, it had a net worth of $79,556.

Another New York outfit in the high-rent district is DISARM, 175 Fifth Avenue, New York, NY 10010. "DISARM has been in the forefront of the campaign for a national firearms policy. DISARM provides a regular distribution of material to members of Congress, provides speakers for the media, public events and debates, and publishes relevant material on firearms controls." Former U.S. Attorney General Ramsey Clark was once chairman and Bob Schwartz was executive director.

THE YWCA CASE

This is the New York story I wish I didn't have to tell. It will make gun owners do a not-so-slow burn. It's the story of the Young Womens Christian Association of the U.S.A. (YWCA), 135 W. 50th Street, New York, Ny 10020. In early 1972 the YWCA's Public Policy Committee studied the issue of gun control and proposed that the full National Board should adopt an anti- handgun statement. The board adopted the statement printed below in October 1972, and directed it to be published in the January 1973 *YWCA Magazine.* Delegates to the YWCA's March 1973 National Convention voted to adopt the statement, which commits the YWCA to support:

". . . federal legislation providing for the licensing of all gun purchasers, users and owners and the registration of all firearms, including ammunition and all other of their component parts; and the banning for production, assembly, sale and possession of all handguns not used for such purposes as law enforcement, military and licensed guard use, sport shooting and hunting."

This meeting prompted the YWCA's Public Policy Center to issue the following statements in its "What Every YWCA Should Know About Gun Abuse" program paper:

"The YWCA believes that model gun legislation would work toward achieving the following specifics:

"Anyone who owns, purchases or uses a gun would possess

a license, the possession of which would be subject to certain regulations determined by federal law. All firearms would be registered. Records would be kept of ammunition and gun component sales, limited to those holding licenses with appropriate gun registration. Gun component parts also include such things as rifle scopes and automatic chokes. There would be no manufacture, assembly, sale or possession of handguns not suitable for purposes as listed above."

The June 1973 *American Rifleman* published an editorial noting the YWCA's adoption of an anti-handgun resolution and noted that, "The Sportsmens Alliance of Michigan . . . has already expressed the view that its members should refrain from contributing to community drives whose proceeds go in part to support the YWCA. Others may follow suit."

Following this NRA article, the YWCA issued a press release claiming that the NRA news item was leading its members to conduct "boycott YWCA" activities. Using any excuse to kick the gunnies around, the anti-gun media began distorting the NRA editorial:

Washington Post: "The *American Rifleman* ran an editorial attacking the YWCA. . . . [T]he sportsmens attack is not simply unfair, it's un-American."

New York Times: "The National Rifle Association and other 'sporting' groups have been propagandizing not only their own members but trade unionists and anyone else they can reach to withhold funds from the YWCA. . . . The tactic is probably too brutal to be effective and the attitude too arrogant to win support."

These two editorials are representative of the media's willingness to trash the NRA for doing things they haven't done. The fact is, there *was* a national boycott organized against the YWCA. But not by the NRA. It was the first national project of a new pro-gun group on the block at the time, the Citizens Committee for the Right to Keep and Bear Arms. The project got started when one of CCRKBA's directors, the late William Loeb, publisher of the *Manchester Union Leader*, ran a full page Citizens Committee ad in his newspaper.

Encouraged by the national media's support of its anti-gun position, the YWCA National Board voted at its May 1974 meeting to join the National Coalition to Ban Handguns as "a further implementation of Convention action in 1973."

According to a YWCA press statement issued on June 19, 1975:

"The YWCA's Public Affairs Program, adopted and amended at succeeding National Conventions, calls for . . . 'the banning of the production, assembly, sale and possession of all handguns not used for such purposes as law enforcement, military and licensed guard use, sport shooting and hunting. . . .'

"We believe that the majority of citizens favor restrictions on gun abuse, and especially the banning of handguns for other than police, security, and sports purposes. . . . But we are alarmed at the growing number of citizens whose use of handguns is based on the simplistic notion that guns provide security against crime and violence. Nothing in our experience or that of other democratic societies supports this contention. On the contrary, a society which attempts to rely on each citizen armed for self-defense or on armed vigilantes is already vulnerable to anarchy."

Apparently, the New York City-nationally-based YWCA doesn't consider it "anarchy" when that city's police department refuses to issue handgun- carrying permits to residents and then wonders why that city annually suffers 1,660 homicides; 3,500 rapes; 96,000 robberies; 170,000 burglaries; and over 100,000 automobile thefts! Even though NYC houses only 3 percent of the entire U.S. population, it disproportionately accounts for 8 percent of all homicides and 17 percent of all reported robberies.

Readers should take note that the Young *Mens* Christian Association (YMCA) has *no* policy statement regarding gun control.

SOUTHWARD IN MEGALOPOLIS

Well, so much for New York. A hop, skip and a jump down Megalopolis we find the Citizens Crime Commission of Philadelphia, 1700 Walnut Street, Philadelphia, PA 19103. "While the Commission supports greater controls over handguns, we are not directly involved in influencing legislation. . . . I am taking the liberty of enclosing some literature from the

National Council to Control Handguns."—CCCP official Ian Lennox, 1977.

RELIGION AS GUN GRABBER

Before we get to Bureaucracyburg-on-the-Potomac, the Nation's Capitol, we have to deal with an aspect of the Gun Grabbers Network that is not strictly geographic. Sadly, it's our religious institutions. What follows should in no way be interpreted as a criticism of any religion or denomination in particular nor of the freedom of religion in general. These are simply objective facts concerning what some of America's religious institutions are saying about gun control.

The American Baptist Convention, Division of Social Concern, adopted in September, 1968, the position: "It is our conviction that a strong gun control law is needed on the national level. We commend those who are working to that end and pledge them our support. . . . We urge that . . . legislation be passed requiring registration of all firearms, the licensing of all owners, and limitation of types of firearms available for private ownership."

Delegates to the Church of the Brethren (Brethren Church) Annual Conference in June 1978 in Indianapolis encouraged stricter handgun controls and called upon its members to relinquish their handguns. The Brethren discourage violence, even in self-defense.

Edgar R. Trexler, editor of *The Lutheran*, which is published by the Lutheran Church in America, Philadelphia, PA, editorialized in the December 1979, issue: "In the long run, is it sensible to expect the lawmakers and the profit-makers to risk defeat at the polls and deficits in their ledgers by rejecting the philosophy of violence that pervades a child's play life in so many homes and is the accepted norm in the community at large? Can we expect a nation to disarm when the people of that nation persistently resist any form of federal gun control and weapons registration?

"How shall we persuade a nation to stop the arms race and find security in mutual trust and peaceful arbitration when the prevailing symbol of security in so·many homes is a pistol on the night table?"

On August 1, 1983, the U.S. Assembly of the General

Conference of the Mennonite Church passed the following resolution:

"WHEREAS non-resistance has formed an integral part of the Anabaptists' understanding of Christ's teaching on which our lives are to be patterned, and

"WHEREAS we see the issue of handgun control as one example of our call to be peacemakers in a world of hatred, alienation and violence,

"THEREFORE be it resolved that we, members of the U.S. Assembly of the General Council of the Mennonite Church, state that it is our belief that handguns are not necessary to the safety or constitutional rights of U.S. citizens.

"In support of the our belief we will take the following action:

"1. Write letters to our federal, state and local elected legislators and executives urging full support for legislative measures to control and limit the sale and ownership of handguns in the United States, except for the use by law enforcement personnel, military and sportsmens clubs.

"2. Work at the local level to promote discussions, seminars, meetings and other educational, informational and legislative means to reduce and eliminate the threat of handgun violence.

"3. Urge all members of the U.S. District and General Conference to voluntarily surrender any handguns in their possession."

(Source: *Gun Week*, September 2, 1983)

In June of 1972, the National Executive Committee of the National Council of Jewish Women, Washington, D.C., adopted a topical statement urging ". . . the federal government, both the executive and legislative branches, to act now to establish a national firearms policy which would require the licensing of all legitimate owners and users of firearms. We urge also that minimum federal standards be established as guidelines for the control of firearms in the States."

On March 26, 1976, it was announced that the Board of Church and Society of the United Methodist Church had adopted the following resolution:

"Therefore, the Board of Church and Society declares its

support for the licensing of all gun owners and the registration of all firearms. Licensing provisions should require adequate identification of gun owners and provide basic standards with respect to age, absence of mental illness, and lack of a serious criminal record. These and other objective standards should be applied in determining the granting or denial of any license.

"In addition, special controls should be applied to the handgun—for it is the most deadly and lest utilitarian weapon in American society. Because the handgun is concealable, it is the weapon of crime; because the handgun is available, it is the instrument used in suicides and crimes of passion.

"Therefore, we call upon the United States government to establish a national ban on the importation, manufacture, sale and possession of handguns and handgun ammunition with reasonable restricted exceptions. . . ."

The Board proposed to partially compensate handgun owners who surrendered their guns.

(Source: Eugene *Oregon Sportsman*, March 26, 1976)

According to the May 1982 issue of the NCBH Handgun Control News, "As part of the [United Methodist] Church NCBH operated as a tax-exempt, tax-deductible organization whose activities were by law restricted to functions of a purely educational nature." Following a ruling by the IRS, NCBH had to disassociate itself from the Church and thereby lost its access to a tax-deductible organization. Nevertheless, "The Board of Church and Society of the United Methodist Church continues to be a member of the [NCBH] Coalition."

The Administrative Board of the U.S. Catholic Conference, 1312 Massachusetts Avenue, N.W., Washington, D.C. 20005, authorized the following resolution on September 11, 1975:

". . . The unlimited freedom to possess and use handguns must give way to the rights of all people to safety and protection against those who misuse these weapons. . . .

". . . We therefore endorse the following steps to regulate the use and sale of handguns:

"1) A several-day cooling-off period. This delay between the time of the sale and possession of the handgun by the purchaser should result in fewer crimes of passion.

"2) A ban on 'Saturday Night Specials.' These weapons are cheap, poorly made pistols often used in street crime.

"3) Registration of handguns. . . . Registration will tell us how many guns there are and who owns them.

"4) Licensing of handgun owners. . . .

"5) More effective controls and better enforcement of existing laws regulating the manufacture, importation and sale of handguns."

(Source: "Handgun Violence: A Threat to Life," U.S. Catholic Conference, September 11, 1975)

Another Catholic body, the U.S. Catholic Conference Committee on Social Development and World Peace, called in early 1978 for a "coherent national handgun control policy," and its governing Board declared that such a policy should include: a cooling-off period of several days between sale and possession of handguns, a ban on licensing of owners and more effective controls on handgun manufacture, sale and importation.

In May 1984, the Catholic Public Policy Commission of Tennessee, Nashville, requested the state legislature to abolish capital punishment, and issued a statement that "we strongly suggest a study of the feasibility of a handgun control measure which authorizes local police to grant licenses for handguns." The police would have the discretionary power in deciding whether or not anyone would be allowed to possess a handgun.

During the past few years several banks around the country have offered forearms as promotional items to prospective depositors. On May 18, 1983 the Ohio Council of Churches adopted the following resolution against the Bank of Findlay, Illinois, which at that time was offering a pair of Colt pistols in lieu of interest:

"WHEREAS the General Board of the Ohio Council of Churches has stood for effective handgun control since May 18, 1976, and

"WHEREAS the unchecked use and flow of handguns as a weapon by the general population contributes greatly to the high number of violent occurrences in our society,

"WHEREAS such actions by entities representing the banking community, such as the current promotional scheme of the Bank of Findlay, Illinois, can be perceived as endorsing the ownership and use of handguns,

"NOW, THEREFORE, BE IT RESOLVED that the General Board of the Ohio Council of Churches deplore the promotional program of the Bank of Findlay, Illinois, and

"BE IT FURTHER RESOLVED that it deplores the widespread advertisement of their program, including the State of Ohio, and

"BE IT FURTHER RESOLVED that the General Board of the Ohio Council of Churches urges all persons of its constituency to refrain from opening deposits in the Bank of Findlay, Illinois, in response to the described promotional program."

(Source: *Gun World*, April 1984, p. 8)

In Washington, D.C., April 1975, an arm of the Union of American Hebrew Congregations ". . . The Commission on Social Action supports the recommendation of the National Commission on the Causes and Prevention of Violence that will eliminate the manufacture, advertising, and sale of handguns except for limited instances where the public order is involved. These exceptions would be exceedingly limited and would include the military, police, security guards and pistol clubs, where they would be kept under secure possession."

In March 1984, Rabbi Bernard Silver, president of the Rabbinical Association of South County, Florida, West Palm Beach, said the RASC is "in support of legislation controlling the sale of handguns. The moral imperative of protecting and sustaining life far supercedes what has been labeled as the right to own weapons."

The following resolution was adopted by greater than a two-thirds vote of the Eleventh General Assembly of the Unitarian Universalist Association, held in Dallas, Texas, June 3, 1972:

"Be it Resolved, that the 1972 General Assembly of the Unitarian Universalist Association recommends uniform gun legislation as follows:

"1. Licensing for the purchase and possession of all useable guns.

"2. Gun registration holding owners legally accountable for all their guns and registrars legally accountable for privacy of records.

"3. Federal, state, provincial and local codes for responsible gun ownership regarding how they are kept, knowledge of proper use and to whom they may be transferred; and

"4. Sound standards for the responsible use of guns by law enforcement agencies.

"5. Restriction of ownership and possession of concealable handguns to persons showing a specific need, such as law enforcement officers and security guards.

"6. Strong legislation forbidding use of 'drop guns' by law enforcement officers."

THE NATION'S CAPITOL

And now, on to Washington, D.C. Our first stop is right across the Potomac River at the National Council for a Responsible Firearms Policy, Inc., 7216 Stafford Road, Alexandria, VA 22307. Because it was founded in 1967—very early in the Gun Grabber game—the NCRFP "virtually pioneered the 'gun control' movement" through the leadership of the late James V. Bennett, former director of the Federal Bureau of Prisons. Its primary Board Member is James B. Sullivan, Minot, North Dakota, while its executive director and acting chairman is David J. Steinberg of Virginia.

The Council has "long advocated a public-awareness campaign of the do's and don't's of safe, responsible possession of firearms by law-abiding citizens." In the past, Steinberg has said of his group in Orwellian double-speak that it is "neither 'pro-gun' nor 'anti-gun,'" yet he supports the Kennedy-Rodino anti-Saturday Night Special bill while contending that the McClure-Volkmer "Firearm Owners Protection Act" is a bill which "thwarts the total public interest by seriously weakening our already inadequate federal firearms-control policy."

The Council continues to be a "viable" organization, if one defines "viable" as a group that issues sporadic news releases every four months or so, although little has been heard of it since mid-1983. Basically, the Council supports the licensing of gun owners and the registration of their handguns.

In a bold and daring move which seems out of place with the slow, gentle manner of his Mount Vernon neighborhood, in March 1983 Steinberg prompted the "Mount Vernon Council of Citizens Associations" to unanimously adopt a mighty and powerful resolution which recommended to community gun owners that they "know how to use [their] gun expertly and safely." If you Tidewater Aristocrats didn't know, you should "learn through expert instruction and keep your qualifications and safety precautions up to date." Yay, Council. Rah! Rah! Rah! Unlike other Gun Grabber organizations, the Council is willing to settle for "milquetoast" victories such as this Mount Vernon non-event.

A year or so earlier, in May 1982, the Council's Steinberg had his sights set somewhat higher. Then, before the U.S. Senate Subcommittee on Criminal Law, it urged "basic support for the Kennedy-Rodino handgun-control bill as the most that could be expected in the foreseeable future—regarding it, however, as inadequate in neglecting violence committed with rifles and shotguns and in compromising excessively even on handguns before the legislative need to compromise was at hand."

Perhaps to steal the thunder of other anti-gun groups, Steinberg has "faulted the handgun-control forces for virtually closing their minds to violence committed with rifles and shotguns," according to his own May 1982 press release.

Steinberg claims that had he been there, he would have voted "no" to banning handguns in Massachusetts in 1976 and in Morton Grove in 1981, as well as voting "no" to Washington, D.C.'s current "freeze" on registering handguns, evidently to keep us guessing.

However, at times Steinberg is refreshingly honest about his goals, unlike most Gun Grabbers. He doesn't attempt to hide his long-range goals by sugar- coating the issue of stronger controls on long guns. In the Council's literature Steinberg has written that he is concerned with:

"The violent misuse of all kinds of firearms and the easy accessibility of all kinds of guns to all kinds of people for all kinds of purposes. . . . Nothing has warranted our modifying the scope of our attention to firearms-related violence. That is, there is no persuasive reason for us to limit our attention to one type of firearm to the exclusion of others.

"Many more handguns than rifles or shotguns are used in

violent crime. But what statistic on long guns are the strictly handgun-control advocates waiting for?. . . . The incidence of all forms of firearms violence is shocking enough. . . ."

Now let's take the 14th Street Bridge into Marbletown itself and see what a nest of Gun Grabbers Washington, D.C. has become. There's just about any type of anti-gun group you can think of in Regulationville. In no particular order, here's a summary:

The Foundation for Handgun Education (FHE), 110 Maryland Ave., N.E., Washington, DC 20002, prides itself on moderation. In mid-1978, FHE President David Gorin, a former past vice-chairman of the NCBH, began to obtain limited media attention for his organization which touts the belief that "the middle-of-the-road approach is the only way the question of handgun regulation will be resolved."

Gorin said, "Our point of view is that control is one option, but that there are others. . . . We would simply like to confront people on both sides of the issue with the facts. We are willing to assume that there are legitimate reasons for people to keep guns—sport and protection, for instance. But they ought to understand that keeping a gun in the nightstand is not intelligent self-defense. It's too dangerous. There's not a police official in the country who would deny that."

FHE was developed to "carve out a middle ground, a position that might find some support in both the gun lobby and the anti-gun lobby." Gorin said. "What we are trying to do is reduce the number of senseless and avoidable killings that take place every year. . . . That's our commitment—not gun control. We think a lot of people who oppose gun control could support a program to eliminate some of these unnecessary deaths and injuries."

FHE's primary activity is publishing *Firearms Litigation Reporter*, a quarterly publication detailing lawsuits seeking to hold handgun manufacturers liable for the criminal misdeed of those who misuse their products. Its editor is Sam Fields, also executive director of FHE and Legal Director of the National Coalition to Ban Handguns.

FHE is a tax-exempt, non-profit organization which strives to reduce handgun- related accidents by "educating the public into understanding that they would be better off without firearms."

At its founding, Richard F. Ware, Jr. was chairman of its Board of Directors.

Among the also-rans of the Gun Grabber Network is the National Gun Control Center (NGCC). After incorporating in March 1976, the NGCC opened an office in Washington, D.C. and proclaimed, "Now the National Rifle Association has competition." Although its director, Joseph J. Levin, Jr. ironically said in an April 1976 interview that "We're not talking about a short-term organization," it ceased operations that August and merged with the National Coalition to Ban Handguns.

But consider a few facts about this group before we bury it in the dustbin of Gun Grabbers Anonymous history.

Its creator was Joseph J. Levin, Jr., a lawyer in Montgomery, Alabama, who had previously served as a legal director of the Southern Poverty Law Center. As Levin believed "Lobbying at the congressional level (for gun controls) is pretty much a waste of effort," he and another lawyer, Morris Dees, nevertheless thought the time was ripe to open up an anti-handgun organization in the Nation's capital.

Dees was one of the defense lawyers for Joanne Little, was national finance chairman for former Governor Jimmy Carter, served in the same capacity for Sen. George McGovern's 1972 presidential bid, and worked with Levin at the Southern Poverty Law Center. Dees claimed, "within five years . . . [we'll] break the National Rifle Association." Sure, Morris.

In an interview with *Southern Outdoors* editor Tom Gresham, Levin said, "I am not for handgun control personally, I am for handgun abolition. Totally and completely." He also said he would "like to see rifles regulated for they can be used for the same purpose as handguns, to knock folks off." When asked what he meant by "regulating," Levin responded: "Maybe sporting clubs could be formed where rifles would be available, or shotguns." He did not think people should be allowed to have long guns in their own home—rifles particularly. "Shotguns I have less concern about." (You figure it out, I can't.)

Fancying themselves specialists in direct mail solicitation,

Levin and Dees used various liberal mailing lists "testing to see if gun control money is available" for their Center.

The Center had the following sponsors: Atlanta Mayor Maynard Jackson; Watergate special prosecutor Archibald Cox; ex-JFK speech writer Theodore Sorenson; LeGrand Mellon of the Pittsburgh Mellon banking family; retired Admiral Gene LaRocque; June Pierson McMichael, executive director of the National Womens Political Caucus; Marjorie Benton of the Chicago Better Government Association; filmmaker Charles Guggenheim; former NYPD Commissioner Patrick Murphy; and U.S. Ambassador to the United Nations Andrew Young.

With sponsors like these, how could their cause possibly fail? By mid-June, Levin was claiming 6,000 members and after mailing out 500,000 packets of literature he projected a membership of "50,000 by summer's end."

According to its D.C. spokesman, John Heath, the eventual aim of the Center was a "complete ban on handguns." Asked if the ban would include sportsmens' guns, he replied that "the details will have to be worked out." Heath, 25, had just graduated from Hartford Trinity College, and after a stint at Common Cause, decided to join the NGCC.

The Center had a sure-fire sales pitch which should have brought the true- blue Gun Grabbers out of the woodwork. After all, how could you miss with visions such as these: "among the education materials and programs the Center says it is planning: literature, cassettes and film documentaries to be distributed to schools, churches, labor unions, civic organizations and other groups; statistics relating to firearms; commercials for radio, TV and print media; a 'National Handgun Turn-In Arsenal' where guns will be stored 'until a Federal gun control law provides either direct compensation or a tax credit to the owners,' " according to the *National Catholic Register*.

"In one of the greatest displays of chutzpah since David took his little slingshot and went out to meet Goliath," according to the *Washington Star*, the NGCC opened its office "to challenge the multimillion-dollar operation of the National Rifle Association a block and a half away." Despite the Biblical analogy, "Johnny's-Got-His-Gun" Levin couldn't pull it off like David did. NGCC died of terminal chutzpah. R.I.P.: March—October 1976.

A Gun Grabber outfit with a little more staying power is the Police Foundation, 1909 K St., N.W., Washington, D.C. 20006. Director Patrick Murphy, former NYPD chief, supports the Kennedy-Rodino anti-handgun bill, which conceivably could ban up to 75 percent of all handgun models currently in production. He said, "We must accept the Kennedy-Rodino bill as a first step toward eventual Federal gun control."

In 1977, the Foundation published *Firearm Abuse* by Steven Brill, which concluded, in part, "The analysis of current local police efforts suggest a need for new approaches to the job of enforcing forearm possession laws."

And now we come to one of the Network's best friends: the United States Conference of Mayors (USCM), 1620 Eye St., N.W., Washington, D.C. 20006. The USCM had been championing the abolition of handguns since its June 1972 national convention when it adopted the following resolution, which reads in part:

"WHEREAS, those who possess handguns cannot be divided into criminals and qualified gun owners; and

"WHEREAS, handguns are not generally used for sporting or recreational purposes, and such purposes do not require keeping handguns in private homes; and

"WHEREAS, the United States Supreme Court ruled in 1939 that firearms regulation is not unconstitutional unless it impairs the effectiveness of the State militia,

"NOW THEREFORE BE IT RESOLVED that the United States Conference of Mayors takes a position of leadership and urges national legislation against the manufacture, importation, sale and private possession of handguns, except for use by law enforcement personnel, military and sportsmens clubs; and

"BE IT FURTHER RESOLVED that the United States Conference of Mayors urges its members to extend every effort to educate the American public to the dangerous and appalling realities resulting from the private possession of handguns, and that we urge the Congress to adopt a national handgun registration law; and

"BE IT FURTHER RESOLVED that (i) effective legislation be introduced and approved by the states not having adequate legislation to that effect; (ii) the proposed legislation shall provide for the registration of all firearms; (iii) state legislation shall require all citizens interested in carrying a weapon to obtain a license after showing just cause and good conduct; (iv) federal legislation shall provide, in addition to existing restrictions, that any person not having a state license to carry a firearm shall commit an offense for transporting such in interstate commerce."

Because of its early involvement in the "ban the handgun" drive, the USCM "trail blazed" the way for future anti-gun organizations. The USCM became the "pathfinder" for other Gun Grabbers: it was the first nationwide organization to actively urge its members to curtail handgun ownership in their communities and showed it meant business by establishing its own full-time, in- house "Handgun Control Staff" (HCS) bureau.

The original Handgun Control Project staff members included Director William R. Drake; Associate Director Joseph D. Alviani; staff associates Lynn Olson and Nancy Loving; with senior staff assistant Patricia Beaulieu. In January 1977 Ms. Loving became director, and Michael Clancy joined as deputy director after having served as a member of the board of directors of People vs. Handguns.

The first significant anti-gun event sponsored by the USCM-HCS was its "National Forum on Handgun Control" held in Los Angeles in May 1977. Anti-gun speeches were presented by Mayor Thomas Bradley (Los Angeles), Mayor Joseph Alioto (San Francisco), Mayor Maynard Jackson (Atlanta), Rep. Robert McClory (Illinois), Attorney General Warren Spannaus (Minnesota), Ian Lennox (executive vice-president of the Philadelphia Citizens Crime Commission), and Sheriff John Buckley (Massachusetts). This meeting brought together many anti-gunners for the first time, which helped form the Network, helped them to exchange ideas for national anti-gun strategy campaigns.

A similar meeting was held the following January in Boston. This meeting's goal was to give "special attention to the formation and activities of state and local handgun control groups. Of special interest were the Massachusetts and California initiative petitions, which seek to place the question of banning handguns on the November 1976 ballot." While Massachusetts voters were to reject a statewide ban, the California measure failed to obtain enough qualifying signatures to even get onto the ballot.

Individuals giving anti-gun presentations included John J. Gunther (USCM executive director); Lawrence Bailey (USCM assistant executive director); Judge J. John Fox (Massachusetts), Ohio State Assemblyman Harry J. Lehman; John Craig (NCCH); Newell Flather (The Blanchard Foundation); Sheriff John Buckley (Massachusetts); Commissioner Robert DiGrazia (Boston Police Department); Dee Helfgott (Los Angeles Coalition for Handgun Control); and Judy Holmberg (People vs. Handguns).

In January 1978, HCS launched a nationwide public-service media campaign, which consisted of two television and three radio Public Service Announcements. The ads cautioned listeners not to possess guns. During the year, the staff did little more than publish its "Targeting In On Handgun Control" monthly newsletter. In November, the U.S. Council of Mayors at its mid-winter meeting "called on President Carter and the Congress to develop legislative and administrative strategies to address the handgun violence problem in the United States." A month later, the HCS released "Television's Action Arsenal: Weapon Use in Prime Time." This study noted that "weapon use on television is excessive and uncomfortably antiseptic. Little blood 'letting' or suffering accompany the weapon use. Thus, the severity of the results of the weapon use are ignored."

After having received "a fifth year of funding from the George Gund Foundation in Cleveland, Ohio," the HCS was able to hold its September 1979 USCM-HSC "National Conference on Handgun Violence" is Washington, D.C. It offered its usual litany of big-name Gun Grabbers: USCM Executive Director John Gunther; Philadelphia Mayor James Tate; Sheriff John Buckley; and D.C. Councilman David Clarke (who wrote that city's handgun-freeze law).

Because it failed to get additional funding from the Gund Foundation, on December 31, 1981, the HCS announced that it had to shut down. Nevertheless, on April 30, 1982, the USCM itself filed an *amicus curiae* brief in a federal appeals court supporting the handgun ban which Morton grove, Illinois had enacted in 1981.

We mustn't forget the American Civil Liberties Union (ACLU) of Washington, D.C. Although the national headquarters is in New York, they're very busy in Washington. On June 28, 1968, the ACLU adopted the following policy statement, which reads in part:

"The ACLU urges adoption of strong federal gun control legislation. . . .

"Effective gun control requires both the registration of firearms and the licensing of owners and dealers. . . .

". . . ACLU urges that any applicant for a gun license be required to demonstrate, by a short test similar to that given for cars and motorcycles, that he knows how to handle a gun with some degree of proficiency. . . ."

The ACLU has not remained completely irrational, however, as shown by their handling of their "participating membership" in the National Coalition to Ban Handguns in the early 1980s. The American Civil Liberties Union announced in June of 1982 that it was formally withdrawing as a "participating member" of the NCBH because it believes that enforcement of a handgun ban could present a threat to civil liberties. But, because it still favors more restrictive gun regulations, the ACLU said that it would become an "affiliate member."

Another citizen group is the Committee for Economic Development and the related Committee for Improvement of Management in Government. "Private importation, distribution, and possession of handguns and parts or ammunition for them should become major criminal offenses under both federal and state laws. The sole owners of such weapons should be the national and state governments, which could then issue them on a temporary and returnable basis to members of the security forces and other authorized persons under carefully drawn regulations. Manufacture should be halted until existing inventories are exhausted, after which further domestic production and export-import trade would be placed under strict licensing controls." Adopted June 1972.

Then, too, there's the ever-present AFL-CIO. In 1971, the AFL-CIO adopted the following policy resolution, which reads in part:

". . . whereas, [it] has been demonstrated by the record of two states which have more stringent laws (New York and Massachusetts) and a number of cities (Philadelphia, Louisville, Toledo, among others). But local gun control laws do not prevent someone from buying a gun in he next town. The answer has to be federal legislation, and. . . .

"Whereas, notwithstanding the NRA lobbying, an overwhelming majority of Americans have indicated they would like to see handgun controls enacted: Therefore, be it

"Resolved, that the AFL-CIO agrees with this sensible majority and strongly urges Congress to enact strong handgun control legislation."

Of course, Common Cause is another Gun Grabber Network affiliate. In a June 1972 statement presented to a U.S. House Judiciary subcommittee, a spokesman said:

"We favor nothing less than total ban on the sale and manufacture of all handguns, with exemption for police, military personnel and pistol clubs, as proposed by Chairman Emanuel Celler and Representative Abner Mikva. And because we agree with Quinn Tamm, the former executive director of the International Association of Chiefs of Police that most persons possessing firearms 'are a menace to themselves and their families,' we endorse the proposal of Senators Hart and Harris that private ownership of handguns also be prohibited."

The National Alliance for Safer Cities on June 26, 1975 released this Executive Council Resolution: "The National Alliance for Safer Cities, Inc, representing 65 national and regional organizations, believes the time has come for effective state and federal gun control. We support the position of the U.S. Conference of Mayors that legislation should be passed to ban the manufacture, sale, importation, and possession of handguns, except to the police, military, and licensed pistol clubs."

The National Association of Attorneys General released this statement of Secretary-Treasurer Frank Bailey in 1975: "The National Association of Attorneys General supports the enactment of restrictive and reasonable legislation applicable to the importation, sale and transfer of all firearms, including rifles and shotguns."

We should take a thorough look at the National Education Association (NEA), 1201 16th Street, N.W., Washington, D.C. 20036. The February 1977 *NEA Reporter* carried the following statement by NEA Executive Director Terry Herndon:

". . . [T]he NEA Representative Assemblies over the past years have taken positions on handgun control. The Assembly in 1974 took this action (reaffirmed by the 1975 Representative Assembly):

"'The National Education Association shall take immediate action to support and lobby for strict gun control that limits the ownership of handguns.'

"In if 1976, the NEA Representative Assembly reviewed this Association policy and made its position more specific. New Business Item 14, as passed by the Assembly, reads:

"'The NEA shall support legislation which attempts to control criminal actions which involve guns through enactment of significant penalties. Such legislation shall also provide prescriptive controls on the manufacturing, distribution, and sale of handguns, with particular efforts to eliminate easily obtained, low-cost handguns, commonly described as Saturday Night Specials.'

"To implement the policies ordered by the Representative Assembly, NEA joined with the National Coalition to Ban Handguns. NEA's Board of Directors recently (December 18, 1976) voted NEA withdrawal from this coalition because many members had expressed their concern that the coalition's positions on handgun control go beyond the NEA

Assembly's mandate. Withdrawal from the coalition, however, will not impair NEA's lobbying for the type of legislation called for by the Representative Assembly. . . ."

In its fair and mature attempt to allow NEA attendees at their July 1978 national convention to discuss the merits of gun control with NRA spokesmen, the NEA initially informed the NRA in March that it *couldn't* obtain a display both at the NEA convention in Dallas. However, following letters of protest by NEA members who were also NRA members, the NEA relented and allowed the NRA to set up a literature booth.

That fall the NEA reviewed its participation policy and announced in April 1979 that it wouldn't allow the NRA to have a literature booth at its Detroit annual convention. The anti-NRA action had been decided by NEA President John Ryor.

In July 1983 the "NEA Legislative Program for the 98th Congress" was adopted by the 1983 Representative Assembly, which included a policy regarding firearms: "Gun control. For the protection of school children and employees and all other citizens, significant penalties should be enacted for criminal actions involving guns with prescriptive controls on the manufacturing, distribution, and sale of handguns."

Another Gun Grabber outfit in D.C. is the National District Attorneys Association" which favors the adoption of legislation to prohibit the manufacture and sale of the cheap, poorly constructed handgun commonly referred to as the 'Saturday Night Special.' "

(Testimony before the U.S. Senate Subcommittee to Investigate Juvenile Delinquency, 1971)

The National League of Cities at its 1971 national convention adopted a resolution advocating a ban on all interstate sales of firearms and a ten-year mandatory sentence for the misuse of a gun during the course of a crime.

Then, following pro-gun pressure, in 1975 it rejected a call for a ban on "small" handguns, but at its 1976 convention it adopted the following anti- gun policies:

1. A ban on the manufacture, sale and possession of handguns having "a combined length and height of 10 inches or

less, with the height being four inches or less and the length six inches or less;"

2. National registration of all firearms;

3. Licensing of all persons desiring to purchase handguns;

4. Deletion of the mandatory penalty for criminal use of a firearm.

The NLC walked into an embarrassing flap in 1979 when it offered the NRA to place an ad in the NLC's annual convention issue of Nation's Cities Weekly, then withdrew its offer. Because the NRA had operated a literature booth at its past three conventions, the NRA automatically received a letter offering it to buy an ad. However, after the NRA bought an ad, the NLC's director of communications, Fred Jordan, rejected the ad because the NRA had repeatedly lobbied the NLC to reject its anti-handgun policy stance. Jordan wrote: "I conclude that the interests of the National League of cities, its members, and the integrity of its policy-making process would not be well served by our publication of your advertising."

Isn't it interesting that NLC's "integrity" was maintained by its suppression of the free speech rights of the gun movement.

There has always been an "environmentalist" facet to the Gun Grabber Network because of people who don't like hunting. The Fund For Animals (FFA) has been fairly typical in its approach to gun control, except during one particular time. The usual "people-are-no-damn-good-but-animals-is-cute-and-cuddly" attitude evidently gave way to sympathy for a fellow human being at least once. Following the murder of singer John Lennon, FFA president and founder Cleveland Amory granted an interview with the *Los Angeles Herald-Examiner*, from which the following quotations are taken:

Q: "Do you think that we as a nation are losing our self-respect in the eyes of the world?"

A: "Of course, and we as a nation will also lose our decency if we allow the death of Mr. Lennon to simply go unanswered. By this, I don't mean just going after the poor creature who did the killing, but also the mental midgets who advocate more and more guns within our society. Such an ignorant position will only mean that the dead will continue to pile up."

Q: "Many people want gun control, yet the NRA has a strong control over Congress. Why is this?"

A: "They have a successful and arrogant lobby. Politicians by the nature of their profession are not very brave, so it's understandable that they refuse to stand up to the NRA."

Another group, while not notable for its great contributions to the anti-gun movement, nevertheless still deserves recognition in the Gun Grabbers Dishonor Roll: the Alliance Against Handguns, PO Box 75700, Washington, D.C. 20013. This group supports enactment of various anti-gun bills.

No discussion of the Gun Grabber Network would be complete without serious consideration of "The Falsely Accused." Gun Grabbers evidently like to cloud the issue by claiming anti-gun support from various organizations which in fact either have no gun policy one way or the other, or which positively support gun ownership. Here are some of the institutions falsely accused of supporting Gun Grabber activities or resolutions—keep in mind that no documented instances of such support can be found for any of the following:

Camp Fire Girls
1740 Broadway
New York, NY 10019
    "We have no policy regarding firearms" control.
    (Source: Letter of April 18, 1978 from CFG national executive director.)

Girls Clubs of America, Inc.
205 Lexington Avenue
New York, NY 10016
    ". . . there has been no policy taken by our National Board on the right to keep and bear arms."
    (Source: Letter of April 11, 1978 from GCA.)

Girl Scouts of the United States of America
830 Third Avenue
New York, NY 10022

"To our knowledge, the Girls Scouts *have never* taken a position on guns, pro or con, and we have no stand one way or the other of gun control or hunting."

(Source: Letter of April 25, 1978 from GSA)

Beer Companies: While rumors are rampant that many beer companies support anti-gun events, again, there is *no* documentation that any American brewery has ever contributed to or co-sponsored any anti-gun function. In fact, a number of key executives of one beer company, the Adolph Coors Brewing Company of Golden, Colorado, supports the Citizens Committee for the Right to Keep and Bear Arms financially.

While not absolutely complete, this is a reasonably thorough overview of the Gun Grabber Network. It should at least give gun owners pause to reflect that there are a lot of "them" out there in America who are out to get all of "us." That's not paranoia speaking, it's plain realism. And this review tells us how important we should regard our own "network" of solidarity in supporting the right to keep and bear arms.

4

Media Mischief

PICK UP ANY NEWSPAPER AND READ how they treat guns. Tune in to any network news broadcast and watch how they treat guns. All too many of us have found that any resemblance between gun-related news reports and actual persons or events is purely coincidental. Part of the reason is that a number of media luminaries are Gun Grabbers themselves. How do we know? Just look in the record books to see who they donate their "hard-earned" cash to.

For example, in the print media, Mary McGrory, columnist with the *Washington Post* who writes regular anti-gun columns, donated $100 to the November 1982 California anti-gun referendum, Proposition 15. In the electronic media, the late Frank Reynolds, ABC newsman, also donated $100 to Proposition 15. No scientific study of "Gun Grabbers In The Media" has been undertaken, but it doesn't take a genius to see that, taken as a whole, the Fourth Estate is just a wee bit biased against guns.

Let's go on with this Proposition 15 media donor list. Take W. E. Chilton III, publisher of the *Charleston Gazette*: he gave $100 to the anti-gun cause. J. Cahill Pfeiffer, former chairman of NBC, also supported Proposition 15, along with Frank Stanton, former president of CBS—no network rivalry there. Richard Reeves, a syndicated columnist, supported Proposition 15 as did Edward Thompson, editor-in-chief of *Reader's Digest*. Incidentally, Proposition 15 was such a touchstone for Gun Grabbers that it will yield us a fascinating look into their political and financial network in our next chapter.

The list of media donors to the Gun Grabbers tells us about where the cause gets some of its money, but money is not what we want to talk about here. Giving money may be the sincerest form of flattery to your favorite cause, but that's not where the real media mischief is done. Media celebrities dispensing anti-gun rhetoric on the opinion page, in the hard news section and on TV news clips are the real problem. Their regular promotion of Gun Grabbing is likely to have far more impact on the outcome of issues in the long run. It's true, their money helps the anti-gun cause, but a few media bucks donated to be spent by known anti-gun groups on political ads doesn't come close to the effectiveness of a famous person telling the public year after year that guns are Bad Things and all us naughty citizens shouldn't own them. Millions of Americans are regularly exposed to such messages, and the non-gun-owning public that's most likely to be influenced has no way of knowing that there's even another side to the story, much less what that other side is.

ADVICE FOR THE GUN-LORN

For example, millions of people read Ann Landers, syndicated social-advice columnist. Every few months she writes an anti-handgun column, but do her readers know that she served on Handgun Control, Inc.'s National Committee or that she personally supported "National Coalition to Ban Handguns Week?" Probably not. Her personal anti-gun connections tend to be invisible. Uninformed readers could easily think Ann Landers was a completely objective journalist simply reporting the social-advice news and telling us The Truth about guns.

In 1984, in a typical anti-gun piece, Ann Landers published a letter from one of her fans who included an article that appeared in the *Arkansas Gazette* which "presents a strong argument for banning handguns." The *Gazette* news item carried the headline "Woman Drops Purse, Gun Fires, Kills Surgeon, 41." The story told of "Dr. Peter R. Dornenburg, 41, an orthopedic surgeon," who "suffered a fatal gunshot wound at a cleaning and laundry firm when a woman dropped a purse containing a pistol and the gun fired. The bullet struck Dr. Dornenburg in the forehead. He died at 6:05 p.m. in St. Vincent Infirmary." The reader who sent in this news clipping signed herself "With You All The Way," and wrote,

"Keep spreading the word, Ann." Then Landers commented, "I suspect the woman, like so many others, bought the gun to 'protect' herself. When are people going to learn that a handgun provides precious little protection in nine encounters out of ten? Wake up, America—heaven only knows how many guns that kill innocent people were stolen from the home of law-abiding citizens who bought them for 'protection.' "

Does Ann Landers ever let you know there's another side? Rarely, and then only in two or three short paragraphs from someone who's so upset at her unfairness that they generally over-react. This, keep in mind, is a standard ploy of anti-gun partisans—to provoke over-reaction and thereby make the opposition look stupid or irrational or both. But on November 5, 1984, a calm, intelligent and rational police chief wrote to Ann and she never bothered to publish his comments. Here, for your edification, is what she wouldn't let you see in her column:

Dear Ann Landers,

I read your column daily in the *Atlanta Journal/Constitution* but never felt the need to write to you until now. Recently you have printed many letters regarding handgun control. I would like to tell the other side of the story.

In March, 1982, Kennesaw, Georgia, passed a mandatory gun ownership ordinance which requires all heads of households to own a firearm—handgun, rifle or shotgun. In 1982, our crimes against persons, which include murder, rape, armed robbery, aggravated assault and residential burglary, decreased 74%. In 1983 these same crimes decreased 46%. So far this year we are showing a further decrease.

I would also like you to be aware that our population has increased in excess of 20% since 1982. We have had no accidents nor incidents involving our citizens with regards to firearms. We attribute this partially to the gun safety course taught on a monthly basis by the police department and partially to the intelligence of our citizens. It is a pleasure to see our senior citizens strolling the streets at night without fear of becoming a victim of a violent crime.

In closing, Ann, I would like to say that we do not advocate every city following our example. This is up to the individual citizen and/or elected official. This has worked for us and we are the only ones we have to please. So in the future, let's look at both sides of the coin.

Sincerely,
Robert L. Ruble, Chief of Police
Kennesaw, Georgia

RECOGNIZING MEDIA BIAS

The problem in "hard news" reports (non-opinion news stories) is worse. Journalists who have personal anti-gun biases infest our American media by the dozen. But sometimes it's difficult to spot the bias. Clever and astute reporters won't admit they're biased and they're shrewd about hiding their biases. They don't beat us over the head with their prejudices. They take pains to look like they're playing it straight. When they write or videotape a gun-related feature, they don't scream and shout, they keep a dead-pan calm and stay objective-looking, but then subtly tilt the wording and emphasis of the story.

Oh, the names are all spelled correctly—most of the time. The reporter's basic "Who, What, Where, When, How" is usually nice and tidy and correct. Reporters are good with the nouns and verbs, but it's the adjectives and the judgement calls that get you. Adjectives are descriptive words like "good" and "bad," but reporters seldom use those nice and simple ones because that would reveal their biases too clearly. And judgement-calls decisively slant the story in favor of some point of view without clearly saying what that point of view is.

Take for example a hypothetical story about a 47-year-old citizen named John Doe walking home from a friend's apartment at 2:15 a.m. on a Thursday night who is accosted at the deserted corner of Lexington and 43rd Street in Manhattan by a teenage mugger named Jim Roe who has come from his Brooklyn tenement home to find rich prey. Let's say the young mugger knocks Doe down, threatens him with a knife, and demands all his money. Further, let's say the citizen finds himself unable to flee to safety and in desperation pulls out his gun and shoots the mugger to death.

Now let's say a reporter from the *New York Daily Dirt* is assigned to the story, and that he privately harbors Gun

Grabber sympathies. His report will describe a middle-aged man who goes by the name of John Doe. After leaving an illicit sexual encounter in the early hours of Friday morning, Doe encountered Jim Roe, a youth who was panhandling on the well-patrolled middle eastside corner of Lexington and 43rd Street. A dispute followed, and at the height of the argument Doe shot young Roe to death with an illegal pistol. The young victim is survived by his mother and two sisters, who live in public housing in nearby Brooklyn.

The preceding two paragraphs are models of slanting a story, the first, to make the shooter sound good—and written to reflect the viewpoint of a mugging victim as closely as possible—the second, to make the shooter sound bad. The basic judgment-call in this story is "Who is the victim?" My description presents John Doe as the victim of a mugging, the hypothetical reporter's story champions Jim Roe as the victim of a shooting. Both examples use color-words throughout to strengthen the judgement-call. I say the shooter is a 47 year old citizen, the make-believe reporter calls him "a middle aged man."I say the shooter is named John Doe, our let's-pretend reporter says the shooter "goes by the name of John Doe." Both descriptions are correct, but they carry a completely different emotional burden.

My statement cites the shooter going home from a visit with a "friend" and our made-up reporter calls it an "illicit sexual encounter." Again, both descriptions may be correct but convey vastly divergent impressions of the shooter. The street corner is described as "deserted" and as "well-patrolled." Again, both are correct: "deserted" refers to the specific time of the incident, "well-patrolled" refers to the general condition of the area. I call Jim Roe a "mugger" and describe specific actions that justify that label. The reportorial version refers to Jim Roe as a "youth" and omits any mention of mugger-like action on Roe's part. I'm sure you can find the other slants for yourself.

But what about those omissions of Roe's aggressive behavior? Can't a pro-gun advocate refute such blatant bias? Probably not. The *New York Daily Dirt* can defend its story because everything they printed is technically correct. The omissions can be defended because only Doe survived to tell the tale and Roe's side of the story will never be known. The knife found at the scene might have belonged to Doe—he was armed with a pistol, wasn't he? And Doe might have just been waiting on that corner to entrap poor Roe because he had been mugged once several years earlier and came to harbor vengeful feelings against young men who stayed out late at night.

So you see, "color-words" in an otherwise technically accurate description can make self-defense with a gun seem somehow disreputable. A person who shoots a criminal can be made to sound less respectable than a defenseless person who gets mugged—or killed—by a criminal. By the time the 90-second TV story or the 10-column-inch newspaper squib is done, the Bad Guy in the story isn't the criminal, it's the crime victim who acted in self-defense.

Most of us can't quite put our finger on the Semantic Pollution in such stories. We can't clearly identify the Gun Grabber bias. Most of us just feel suspicious of the media and wish things were more clear-cut. But clear-cut writing is just what the biased reporter wants to avoid. It's easy to hide behind the cliche that "actual events are too complicated to paint in black and white." Such cliches only serve to hide editorial opinion in hard news stories where it does not belong. It is through this Invisible Veil of Bias that the media wield such tremendous power. Victor Lasky, a columnist and author of more than average perceptiveness calls the media "the most powerful institution in America today."

THE RIGHT TO SELF-DEFENSE

Here, to help break the grip of that media power, are the facts about self-defense. Self defense: what are your rights? It's a question of growing importance. More and more self-defense cases are appearing in the media. A plumber in Chicago, confronted by youths with a knife and a gun, drew his own gun. A so-called "Lone Ranger" in Los Angeles broke up a robbery and killed an armed thug. A New Yorker shot four "youths" on a subway train. Each claims he acted in self-defense. What does the law say?

If you started the fight, if you're where you have no right to be, if you could back away, or if you could protect yourself with less than deadly force, then your right to shoot someone else may depend on what state you live in. And in the final analysis, your fate may depend on how sympathetic your jury is.

A book by Frederick and Joan Baum called the *Law of Self-Defense* provides some general guidelines for the concerned gun owner. According to the Baums, a person claiming to act in self defense must meet certain tests.

You must not have started the fight or continued it after the attacker was ready to give up.

You must honestly believe that you are in imminent danger of death, serious injury or some serious crime such as rape, robbery or arson, and you must honestly believe that nothing less than deadly force is sufficient.

And you must have a reasonable basis for your beliefs.

In some states, you must retreat as far as you safely can before firing.

Obviously, self defense can get very complicated. The Associated Press in 1985 released a news feature on self defense cases that was actually helpful for a change. Despite the complications, there are some legal protections for the person who claims self defense. AP writer Robert Barr noted an observation in a Supreme Court opinion by Justice Oliver Wendell Holmes, who said, "Detached reflection cannot be demanded in the presence of an uplifted knife."

Not only do courts refuse to demand detached reflection in emergencies that provoke self defense, but juries in New York are also often instructed to consider what they would have done if they had been the defendant. The Associated Press mentioned first the case of Bernhard Goetz, New York's "subway gunman" who was indicted in late March, 1985, on four counts of attempted murder. In this case, a crucial question is whether he reasonably believed four youths were about to attack him.

In this case, two Grand Jury hearings were held, the first resulting in only concealed weapons charges and the second in the attempted murder charges. The self defense claim will be heard by a jury.

In Los Angeles, a 69-year-old man named Cornell Smith was sitting in his truck at Tam's hamburger stand on December 9th of last year when he saw two men robbing a customer. Smith grabbed his pistol and yelled "Don't do it," according to Los Angeles Police Department Detective Tony Sanchez. Sanchez said, "One of the men turned and it looked like he was going to shoot, so Smith shot him."

Smith disappeared "like the Lone Ranger," police said, but he surrendered several days later. Deputy District Attorney Robert Lord concluded, "Smith was stopping a robbery."

In this case, Smith's claim of self defense prevailed: he was not charged with any offense.

On New Year's Eve in a Beverly Hills elevator, 81-year-old Thomas Korshak and his wife were confronted by a robber. The robber held his hand in his jacket pocket as if he had a gun pointed at the elderly couple.

Korshak pulled his own .38 caliber revolver and shot the man three times. When police came to investigate the case, it was discovered that the robber did not have a gun. As it turned out, that made no difference. Korshak reasonably believed he was and his wife were in imminent danger and there was no place to retreat to. Korshak was only charged with a misdemeanor for carrying a loaded firearm in public and was placed on probation.

A New Jersey case illustrates that shooting in self defense may be a right that you have some of the time but not all of the time. Manuel Marin discovered two burglars in his kitchen on December 8th, 1981. When Marin confronted them and fired one shot, the burglars ran outside. Marin moved to a window and fired two more rounds as the screaming burglars ran for their car.

Manuel Marin was charged on two felony counts of aggravated assault. Authorities said that he had a right to fire the first shot in his kitchen, but no right to fire the last two shots because the burglars represented no further threat to him or his home. Marin was placed in a special program for first offenders, in which he admitted no guilt and did not go to trial.

Even in the same incident, some shots may legally be fired in self defense while others may not. When it comes to self defense, it pays to know your rights, especially with the media's general disregard of their educational obligations.

THE GOETZ CASE

No account of Gun Grabber bias in the media would be complete without a bow to the startling phenomenon of Bernhard Goetz and the rise of "Thug Buster" sentiment in the American public. Goetz, widely known as the "Subway Vigilante," has been charged with attempted murder in the December 22, 1984, shooting of four young men who accosted him in a subway train and demanded money.

The Goetz case has aroused public opinion in America as few shooting incidents ever have, and the overwhelming majority has come down squarely on Goetz's side. By all indications, the public sees Goetz as having acted properly in self-defense within his moral and legal rights. His arrest and booking for attempted murder have outraged many law-abiding citizens who see Goetz as having done what every good citizen ought to do: stopping violent criminals in no uncertain terms.

The facts of the case are reasonably clear: On the afternoon of December 22, 1984, Goetz was a passenger in a subway car in lower Manhattan along with some 20 others. Witnesses say that four young men in the car were acting in a rowdy, intimidating manner. The four approached Goetz and told him to give them five dollars. Goetz replied, "I have $5 for each of you," and fired five times with a .38-caliber handgun, wounding all four, two in the back. One of the young men, Darryl Cabey, 19, was shot in the spine, paralyzed from the waist down. Goetz fled and later turned himself in to police in Concord, N.H.

One of the most astonishing facets of the Goetz case has been the relative lack of bleeding-heart hand-wringing one might expect to hear for the young thugs who got shot—even though all four were black and Goetz is white. Very few editorial writers trotted out the old liberal shibboleths such as "Those who approve of this shooting think it's fine for a white man to shoot black men." Jimmy Breslin of the *New York Daily News* was one of the few. But for the most part, the traditional racial and partisan divisions of the past simply haven't appeared in the Goetz case.

Despite the fact that Cabey had been seriously wounded

and is listed in critical condition, there appears to be very little if any public sympathy for him. A white New York City radio personality even said that if Goetz had known how to use his gun properly, all four young muggers would be dead. Many black people feel the same. *Time* magazine quoted Roy Innis, chairman of the Congress of Racial Equality, as saying that Goetz was "the avenger for all of us," and "Some black man ought to have done what he did long before. I wish it had been me." Innis also offered to raise defense money for Goetz, according to *Time*.

James Q. Wilson, author of *Thinking About Crime* and professor of government at Harvard thinks the reason that liberals haven't spoken up for the young muggers is that there aren't any more in New York: they've all been mugged. Wilson may have a point. New York's strict handgun ban that took effect in August, 1980, is a colossal failure: now only outlaws have guns. The disarmed public feels helpless because the police can't control crime. When Goetz shot those four young muggers, the response one hears on the street is that he did exactly what every New Yorker wanted to do.

Immediately after his arrest, Bernhard Hugo Goetz, a 37-year-old engineer, was represented by New York attorney Frank Brenner. Brenner then withdrew from the case citing "irreconcilable differences with Mr. Goetz over how his defense should be conducted." Goetz hired two new lawyers, Joseph Kelner, a past president of the American and the New York State Trial Lawyers Association, and Barry I. Slotnick, an attorney with wide experience in criminal trials. The two said January 15, 1985, that their client was not a "vigilante."

Strictly speaking, is Goetz a vigilante? Webster's authoritative Third International Dictionary gives as the sole definition of *vigilante*: a member of a vigilance committee—which Goetz is assuredly not. *Vigilance committee* in its turn is defined as: a volunteer committee of citizens for the oversight and protection of an interest; *especially* a committee organized to suppress and punish crime summarily (as when the processes of law appear inadequate).

This is more to the point. In a place with a crime problem like New York City, it shouldn't surprise us that "the processes of law appear inadequate" to many New Yorkers.

What's surprising is the absence of genuine vigilance committees and genuine vigilantes. But since there are no vigilance
committees in New York for Goetz to belong to, it's inaccurate to call him a vigilante. We can still ask, "Did he take the
law into his own hands?" But is that what vigilante means? An
interesting quibble.

Mr. Kelner said in his statement that Mr. Goetz had acted
"reasonably and understandably in a life-threatening situation
with money being demanded of him." The word "reasonably"
is a reference by Mr. Kelner to New York State's law on
self-defense. It says a person may use deadly force if it is
necessary to defend himself against the "imminent use of
unlawful physical force" and if he "reasonably believes" that
the other person is committing or attempting to commit a
robbery and that safe peaceable withdrawal is impossible.

Kelner and Slotnick issued a written statement that they
said reflected Mr Goetz's "thoughts and beliefs" in the case.

In it Goetz, who helped to prepare the statement, said he
hoped that his "ordeal" would focus public attention on crime
and that his case would result in better protection for people
who travel on the subways. He thanked the many people who
had expressed "their understanding and support" and said the
many letters he had received dealt with four main themes:

1. Americans are frustrated and angry that they must live in
constant fear of crime.

2. Crime has taken possession of our lives.

3. New ideas are needed to prevent crime.

4. Changes must be made in our laws and law enforcement
to deal with the crime problem.

Mr. Kelner, himself the victim of an assault 18 months ago
outside his New York City law office, said, "we are proud and
privileged to represent him in this great cause that affects the
safety and welfare of all Americans". Mr. Kelner said he
would donate his services. Mr. Slotnick said he would not.

The Goetz phenomenon has raised interesting social questions in the media. Articles have been written with the following theme: Citizens who have willingly yielded the administration of vengeance to the state are now looking at Goetz as a
model of their own feelings. Many feel that the social contract
in America has broken down. They are saying to the state,

"You've defaulted on your end of the social contract. Now I revoke mine."

On the streets of New York, "Thug Buster" T-shirts became hot-selling items in the wake of the Goetz shooting. They bear the red barred circle of the International Negative Symbol and a line drawing of a crook instead of a spook where you've seen it in the logo for the box office smash *Ghost Busters*. Beneath the cutesy emblem are the printed words: ACQUIT BERNHARD GOETZ.

Walter Berns, a political scientist at Washington D.C.'s American Enterprise Institute, says about public response in support of Goetz and anger at his arrest, "Anger, coming from someone who has not been personally victimized by a criminal, is an expression of concern for fellow citizens. That expression should not be derided or despised."

The media have not explored in any depth the backgrounds of the four young men shot by Bernhard Goetz in the highly publicized Manhattan subway incident. As mentioned above, on the afternoon of December 22, 1984, Goetz was a passenger in a subway car in lower Manhattan along with some 20 others. Witnesses say that four young men in the car were acting in a rowdy, intimidating manner. The four approached Goetz with sharpened screwdrivers and told him to give them money. Goetz allegedly replied that he would give them money and then fired five times with a .38-caliber handgun, wounding all four, two in the back. Goetz fled and later turned himself in to police in Concord, N.H.

CUDDLY "YOUTHS"

Here, provided by Sgt. Ron Severin of the Public Information division of the New York Police Department are some historical facts on the four individuals shot by Bernhard Hugo Goetz. These facts come from documents called rap sheets in police jargon and could have material bearing on whether Goetz had reason to fear for his safety:

James Ramseur, DOB (date of birth) 8/15/66. (18 years old at the time of the subway shooting.) 6 arrests, 5 for petit larceny, one for burglary in the 3rd degree, criminal mischief and damaging property. Tried in 1983 on the burglary, mischief and damaging charges, plea bargained, entered a guilty plea to a lesser offense, convicted of criminal trespass in the 2nd degree, sentence not noted. Convicted in 1983 on charges of petit larceny, sentenced to 60 days (served). Various bench warrants for failure to appear in court. On Friday, June 28, 1985—six months after Goetz shot him— Ramseur was arrested by the New York Police Department on charges of raping and robbing a 20-year-old woman on May-5 of 1985. The charges included rape, robbery, sodomy, assault and criminal possession of a deadly weapon in the attack at a New York City apartment complex.

Barry Allen, DOB 1/10/66 (18 in 1984). 5 arrests, 1 for assault in 1982, convicted of assault, sentenced to probation; 1 for burglary; 1 for criminal mischief; 1 for possession of burglary tools; 1 for reckless endangerment of property. Tried in 1982 on the criminal mischief charge, which included counts of petit larceny and possession of burglary tools, plea bargained, convicted of a lesser offense, disorderly conduct. Sentence not noted. Bench warrants for failure to appear in court.

Troy Canty, DOB 9/9/65 (19 in 1984).6 arrests, 5 convictions; 1 arrest for felony possession of stolen property 1/27/82, plea bargained, convicted of lesser offense, disorderly conduct, sentence not noted; 2 arrests for petit larceny, 4/17/82 and 4/29/82—in the second petit larceny case, which included charges of possession of stolen property, entered guilty plea to possession of stolen property, sentence not noted; 1 arrest for possession of burglary tools, petit larceny, criminal mischief, and damage of property, plea bargained, convicted of lesser charge, petit larceny, sentence 20 days (served); 1 arrest for burglary in the 3rd degree, possession of burglary tools and possession of stolen property, 11/9/83, entered guilty plea to petit larceny misdemeanor, sentence 30 days (served). Bench warrant for failure to appear in court on 1/12/84 charges of petit larceny and criminal mischief.

Darryl Cabey, DOB 1965 (19 in 1984). Rap sheet sealed by court order in connection with the Goetz case. *Time* magazine reported the details of at least one Cabey arrest before the case was sealed. A bench warrant had been issued for Cabey's arrest for failure to appear in court on charges of robbing three men with a shotgun. News sources say but cannot confirm that earlier arrests and at least one conviction on Cabey's rap sheet were sealed before the public had a chance to learn the details about them.

Time magazine calculated that between them, the four young men have nine convictions, twelve outstanding cases and ten bench warrants for non-appearance in court.

Goetz could not have known of these facts when he was accosted by the "youths" on that subway. However, it is difficult to believe that four "youths" with these backgrounds would not reveal their character in some way by their behavior on that subway, which Bernhard Goetz could have seen, heard and felt.

Of course, these facts were shrugged off in ABC News' unprecedented full hour "20/20" presentation on the Goetz case in the spring of 1985. While pretending to be fair, as in the *New York Daily Dirt* example above, "20/20" correspondent Geraldo Rivera—whose real name is Gerald Rivers—does his best to discredit Goetz in general and guest talking head Arthur Miller, Harvard's noted Constitutional law expert, flatly rejects Goetz's self-defense contention. Nowhere in the whole hour does any ABC News reporter lend any credence to anything Goetz said or did.

What viewers saw was a reconstruction with actors of the scene last December when Goetz shot the four "youths"—of course, it has to be "youths," not "muggers," "muggers" is too judgmental a word for us "objective" Gun Grabbers. The reconstruction was based on accounts by three of the wounded youths and the two-hour video-taped confession Goetz made to law officers when he surrendered in Concord, New Hampshire, nine days after the shootings. ABC viewed the tape but did not broadcast it, instead dubbing only parts of the audio track, which was the first time the public heard any segment of the confession.

The reconstruction was intended to show spatial relationships, according to ABC News executive producer Av Westin, which may shed light on Goetz's feeling that his life was in danger. Westin said the actors representing the subway riders acted in "neutral" ways. They all wore blue coveralls. A gun was pointed, but it was never fired in the re-enactment. Just think how realistic this "reconstruction" was. How

116

"neutral" do you suppose Troy Canty and Barry Allen and James Ramseur and Darryl Cabey—up on shotgun robbery charges—were *really* acting in that subway car? But that's the media for you: they manufacture a fictitious "neutral" dramatization that supposedly gives us a "rationalized" and "objective" look into the "real" situation, when the scene to me seems obviously cooked up to show the young muggers in the best possible light. ABC News got away with it because they can claim that they "neutralized" their "Goetz" actor too by not having any shot fired from his gun. You don't have to be an Einstein to realize which of the two sides comes off best in such a rigged pseudo-documentary situation. A "rationalized" Goetz could only lose his fear, while sanitized muggers lose all trace of aggression and threat; the muggers look nice and the Goetz actor looks cold and calculating. Media mischief at its most refined.

Then "20/20" brings on Arthur Miller, the feisty law professor, who examined Goetz's movements and whether deadly force was a reasonable response every step of the way. In the reconstruction, Miller examines whether Goetz was provoked, whether he could have retreated and whether deadly force was the only remaining recourse. Through a step-by-step freeze-frame study of the re-enactment, Miller concludes that Goetz probably was not afraid for his life at every stage. Miller also very strongly disputes the self-defense defense of Goetz. Where was the opposing hotshot law professor to rebut Miller? Not on "20/20," you can be sure.

ABC News also showed new footage of Goetz shot by ABC in his apartment. Goetz permitted the camera session but refused interview requests from Rivera and Barbara Walters on the advice of his counsel.

However, Troy Canty and James Ramseur—who was arrested, remember, on charges of rape and robbery six months after the subway shooting—and Shirley Cabey, mother of Darryl Cabey, the most seriously wounded "youth"—we must remember that Cabey is a "youth," not a "thug," even if he did hold up three men with a shotgun—eagerly accepted invitations to be interviewed. They were all "just folks." We didn't see their rap sheets. It was almost as realistic as *The Wizard of Oz*. There was also what Av Westin called "exclusive video" of Cabey in his hospital bed, taken by Cabey's brother. Westin said, "There's a value in seeing the victim of this shooting." Westin didn't say what the value was. (What else could the value be than to prejudice people against Goetz's self-defense plea?)

"20/20" has done full hour shows on single subject before, for example, cancer and drug running, but this is the first time the broadcast has devoted its entire time to a current news story. Why did they do it? Could Geraldo Rivera be a Gun Grabber? Or his fellow correspondents? Or his producers and directors and his network executives? Oh, heaven forbid! They're just objective reporters doing their job. It's nasty work, but somebody has to do it. That's what the *New York Daily Dirt* says, too. Well, in Geraldo Rivera's case I have first-hand knowledge that he's a Gun Grabber. I did a radio show in Chicago on the ABC affiliate station WIND to promote my earlier book *The Rights of Gun Owners*. Rivera was the guest on the show just before me. He knew I was next and he knew who I was. Coming out of the studio he made a number of anti-gun remarks to me. He should at least have the honesty to announce himself as an anti-gun advocate rather than an objective reporter while he's on the air.

We can't let this chapter end on a completely cynical note. There are some interesting things the media do in the public interest. Here's one: believe it or not, there's a song about Bernhard Goetz on a music video. An independent group associated with Manhattan's Center for the Media Arts has produced a video entitled "The Subway Vigilante," centered around an encounter between a citizen and four punks. The video rock generation watched the dramatized shootout set to these inspired lyrics: "He's the subway vigilante, he's tired of being had. Don't bother with him brother, he'll get you if you're bad. Don't come across like a tough guy, though he looks so calm and quiet. He'll pull his .38 out and serve you bullets if you try it." Well, the rhyme scheme is not exactly Shakespeare, but it gets the point across. Music videos could be a whole new threat to the Gun Grabbers.

5

Anti-Gun Politics
Equals Big Money

ANYWHERE YOU LIFT THE COVER OF THE Gun Grabber Network you find money. And politics. Of course, it couldn't be any other way. If your goals include voting away the freedoms of your fellow citizens, as the Gun Grabbers' do, you're engaged in politics by definition. And everybody knows that politics costs money. So in this chapter we'll examine the basic fact of Gun Grabber life: Finance and politics are inseparable from the movement.

Yes, it's true of *any* movement, not just the Gun Grabbers. Call it sad or call it funny, politics could be termed the process of getting the best government money can buy. However, it's not my purpose to comment on movements and politics, but to protect the interests of gun owners. And gun owners have a special interest in this particular financial-political process: Gun Grabber money and Gun Grabber politics could mean the end of the rights of gun owners forever. Thus, we must lift the cover from the Gun Grabber movement and see how the money—the lifeblood—flows to nourish the politics.

So where do the Gun Grabbers get their money? And what do they do with it once they've got it? If there's a short answer, it's this: Gun Grabber money comes primarily from wealthy businesspeople and celebrities and it goes primarily to politicians and Gun Grabber organization operations. But if you want the long answer, hold on to your Stetsons: you're in for a wild roller- coaster ride into Gun Grabber Moneyland.

Ferreting out *all* the Gun Grabber money in America would be impossible. But the public record gives us a sharply delineated profile of Gun Grabber fat cats. The most reveal-

119

ing records come from two prime sources: 1) the paperwork left behind by the hugely unsuccessful California campaign to ban handguns in November 1982 known as Proposition 15, and 2) the Federal Elections Commission file of *Handgun Control, Inc.* Political Action Committee (HCI-PAC) receipts and disbursements for the federal elections of 1982 and 1984.

PROPOSITION 15

If passed, *Proposition 15* would have allowed state residents to possess only those handguns which were legally registered with the state during a set time period. Although ownership of these registered guns could be transferred to new buyers, no new handguns could be transferred to new buyers, no new handguns could have been imported into, manufactured in or registered in the state after mid-1983. The final tally on Proposition 15 was 2,840,154 for, 4,799,596 against—gun control lost by a 2 to 1 vote. Here are profiles of some of those who paid top-dollar to lose:

The American Federation of State, County and Municipal Employees, a government workers union with lobbyists in Washington, D.C. gave $500.

Gerson Bakar, chairman of the San Francisco real estate development firm Gerson Bakar & Associates, gave $3,500.

C. Minor Barringer, an individual living in Chadds Ford, Pennsylvania, gave $5,000.

Giles H. Bateman, executive vice-president and chief financial officer of San Diego's Price Company—a wholesaler of appliances, food, liquor and restaurant, automotive and hardware supplies with annual sales over the billion dollar mark—gave $2,500.

William Belzberg, chairman and president of the Beverly Hills real estate development and investment firm First City Properties Inc., gave $1,000. First City Properties Inc. has 90 employees and revenues of $59.7 million.

Blue Chip Stamps of Los Angeles gave $1,000.

Wallace W. Booth, chairman, president and chief executive officer of Ducommun Incorporated, a Los Angeles distributor of electronic components, manufacturer of hydraulic fittings, and provider of metal forming and chemical milling services, gave $1,200. Ducommun has revenues of $304 million.

Elizabeth P. Borish, an individual living in Vermont, gave
$5,000.

British Motor Car Distributors of San Francisco gave $100
as did the California Federation of Teachers.

A STRANGE TALE

The *Buckeye Trust*—ah, the Buckeye Trust! This is quite a
story. In brief, *Gun Week* executive editor Joseph Tartaro and
his intrepid crew cost *Handgun Control, Inc.* a $40,000 con-
tribution from the Buckeye Trust of Ohio that was earmarked
for Proposition 15. If twisty-turny plots and byzantine ma-
chinations bore you, skip to the next listing. But if you want
one of the most educational examples imaginable of Gun
Grabber hijinx, read on.

It all started out innocently enough: The November 5, 1982
issue of *Gun Week* ran a Page 2 story headlined *Sinatra,
Others Support Proposition 15* (we'll get to Sinatra in our
chapter on The Non-Shooting Stars). It was essentially a list of
Gun Grabber moneybags released by California's Fair Political Practices Commission, with a few barbed comments
thrown in for good measure. In the next-to-last paragraph
Gun Week stated: "Contributions received through Handgun
Control Inc. also included Phillip Schlichting, a vice president of the Goodyear Bank in Akron, Ohio, $40,000. . . ." All
very simple and straightforward journalism: HCI was acting
as the intermediary for a very large donation from a bank
official. The report was based on public records.

Very shortly Schlichting contacted *Gun Week* from Akron
and complained to Legislative Editor Jim Schneider: "Your
story is wrong. I'm just calling *Gun Week* to indicate my
disapproval of that kind of activity if the facts aren't right—
and they aren't." Schlichting claimed he was not the source of
the funds, but had merely signed the check. He was upset
because the *Gun Week* story had caused some backlash:
"What this has caused at the local level," said Schlichting, "is
I've heard there is a possible boycott of the bank. There are
all kinds of people who are just coming off the walls. I don't
need a boycott and all the rest of it."

Editor Schneider, being a conscientious journalist, duly
contacted the California commission that had released the

information and asked why they handed out bum facts. A commission official, Special Assistant John Meade, told Schneider the commission must have received incorrect information from *Handgun Control, Inc.*, because it said right here in black-and-white on the HCI report that Schlichting was the donor." That's how it was reported by HCI, who originally collected the money and made the contribution," Meade told *Gun Week's* Schneider. "If Schlichting is not indeed the source of the contribution, he should have been listed here as an intermediary, not as a contributor, which is how he's listed. When you call Mr. Schlichting back, you'd better tell him he's in violation of California law and a correction has to be made."

So, editor Schneider called back banker Schlichting in Akron and gave him the bad news. A few days later, Schlichting returned the favor and told Schneider that he had informed HCI that there was an error in their reporting and he considered the matter closed—of course, not saying who the real donor was. However, when the California commission released its final report on Proposition 15 on March 30, 1983—some four months after the last phone call—Schlichting was still listed as the donor of the $40,000. Editor Schneider called the commission to see if they had simply failed to make the correction, but was told that they had received no correction. Things were getting curious.

By now, it seems, the California commission was upset. Commission spokesman Lynn Montgomery looked into the matter and in May the California Attorney General sent a letter asking for the correct information about who gave the $40,000. Long wait. Finally, on July 19, Goodyear Bank— which in the meantime had changed its name to National City Bank—sent a letter signed by vice-president Robert A. Holop saying that the $40,000 came from the Buckeye Trust. But what the hell was the Buckeye Trust?

Editor Schneider couldn't find out. Trusts are pretty esoteric things that most of us know little about. And there's not much in the way of public records on trusts. After extensive and fruitless research, *Gun Week's* Schneider called Ohio State Representative Richard Rench (R-Milan) and asked if he knew anything about Buckeye Trust. Rench said he didn't, but since a number of his constituents were interested in where that $40,000 came from, he'd look into it. So Rench called National City Bank's Holop. Holop's secretary said he was on vacation. She suggested that the legislator talk to David Wilson of Buckingham, Doolittle & Burroughs of Akron, attorney for Buckeye Trust. So Rench called Wilson. Wilson gave Rep. Rench the red carpet treatment: "I don't have any obligation to discuss this matter with you. You sound like you're the NRA after me." Curiouser and curiouser.

Rep. Rench relayed his lack of success to *Gun Week*. Nothing daunted, editor Schneider asked Rick Story of the Wildlife Legislative Fund of America—headquartered in Columbus—if he'd help. Story checked the Charitable Foundations Section of the Ohio Attorney General's Office. Lo! and behold. The Buckeye Charitable Lead Trust, also known as the Thomas W. Roush Charitable Lead Annuity Trust, was indeed listed. But what the hell was the Buckeye Charitable Lead Trust?All editor Schneider had now was a longer name and an alias. The suspect was still a mystery.

Gun Week ran into stone walls everywhere. Nobody knew who was behind the Buckeye Charitable Lead Trust. So the publication turned to institutional sources, the *Taft Foundation Reporter* and the *Foundation Directory* published by New York's Foundation Center. Both listed only one Roush Foundation, and it was in Akron. Verrry interesting. But it was called simply The Roush Foundation, and the directory entry said it had formerly been called the Galen A. Roush Foundation. No mention of Thomas W. Roush or Buckeye. *Gun Week* up to this point had performed a classic job of investigative reporting, but now made an assumption based on scanty facts—incorrectly, as it turned out—that The Roush Foundation was the suspect. And the directory listings on the Roush Foundation told all.

So, in the September 23, 1983 issue, *Gun Week* reported—incorrectly, keep in mind—that directors of Buckeye Trust included officers of *Roadway Express, Inc.*, one of the country's 25 largest transportation companies with 19,000 employees—its holding company, Roadway Services, Inc. has revenues of $1.25 billion.*Gun Week* reported that Galen

Roush, owner of Roadway Express, and his wife Ruth established the Galen A. Roush Foundation in 1967. The only trouble was, the Galen A. Roush Foundation was neither the Thomas W. Roush Foundation nor the Buckeye Trust. However, since there was no public information on the actual suspect, *Gun Week* had no way of knowing that.

Gun Week's story raised a firestorm of complaints to Roadway Express from many companies connected with the firearms industry for donating the $40,000 to HCI. Roadway Express officials were horrified. They claimed they knew nothing about any such contribution. They looked into the matter and for some strange reason got instant cooperation from Buckeye Trust's legal representatives where *Gun Week* and Rep. Rench could not. Things were getting positively weird.

On October 4, 1983, attorney Richard A. Chenowith of Buckingham, Doolittle & Burroughs of Akron sent the following note to Charles F. Zodrow, chairman of the Board of Roadway Express:

"Dear Chuck,

"The Buckeye Trust is a charitable Trust, of which The Goodyear Bank was Trustee in 1981 and 1982, when the contributions were made to *Handgun Control, Inc.*

"The Trustee had the sole discretion in choosing this beneficiary, but it turned out that Handgun Control, Inc., was a beneficiary not permitted by the Trust instrument. Handgun Control, Inc. has therefore agreed to return the entire contribution, and it has already returned $10,000.

"When you respond to the complaints you have had, you may also want to emphasize that neither you nor any other Roadway executive or Director is connected with The Buckeye Trust or has any power to direct or influence its actions."

Now this is a most remarkable note for several reasons. Just a month earlier, recall, the same law firm's David Wilson had told a state legislator, Rep. Rench, to in effect go take a flying leap. Records began to surface that proved the Thomas W. Roush Foundation (the real Buckeye Trust) was created in 1966 by Mrs. Ruth Roush, wife of Roadway's owner Galen Roush. Dr. Thomas W. Roush, foundation namesake, sits on the board of directors of The (other) Roush Foundation and *both trusts are based on Roadway stock.* Why didn't the lawyer's note to Roadway chief Zodrow mention those facts? Was it because those facts were common knowledge to all Roadway executives? Then too, why would the Buckeye Trust's lawyer be giving free friendly advice to Roadway's boss? Very peculiar, and we'll soon see why.

Then on October 24, chairman Zodrow sent Roadway division vice-presidents this inter-office memorandum:

"In order to clear up the false information that has recently been printed in some sportsmen publications regarding Roadway Express' alleged support of anti-gun issues, I want to provide you with the background information to set the record straight.

"First, the Buckeye Trust is a charitable trust with a local Akron bank as the sole trustee. Upon termination of the trust, a number of years in the future, the remainder of the trust will go to one of Mr. Roush's children.

"Upon investigating the alleged contribution in support of Proposition 15 in California I discovered (1) that a contribution of $40,000 was in fact made by Buckeye Trust to Handgun Control, Inc, and (2) such a contribution was not authorized by the trust agreement creating the Buckeye Trust.

"As a result, the bank trustee has demanded the return of the contribution from Handgun Control, Inc. A portion of the contribution has already been returned and they have agreed to return the remainder to the Buckeye Trust.

"While the above are the facts that I have been able to determine, I want to emphasize that I am not a director, officer, or in any way related to the Buckeye Trust. Nor is any other director or officer of the company in a position to have any power to direct or even influence the trust's actions.

"While the company does, from time to time, make charitable contributions, such contributions are related educational, youth, health, or similar type organizations. They are intended to support the communities in which our employees work and are certainly not intended to create controversy or to erode our customer base.

"The damage done to our business by the error of a local trust officer here in Akron, who is not now nor at any previous time been related to or worked for Roadway, was certainly not forseen by him. However, I hope that the above information will assist you in overcoming the damage that has been done."

Another note came from Lisle M. Buckingham, a partner of the law firm Buckingham, Doolittle & Burroughs—and a director of Roadway Express: "Mr. Zodrow is not a director of any trust that has donated funds to the anti-gun element and neither have I. I have owned guns since I was 12 years of age and still have a shotgun, rifle and Colt revolver and, consequently, I am not anti-gun."

Yay. Hooray. Underwhelming. That supposedly ended the matter. *Gun Week* published those facts along with retractions of its error. The $40,000 donation to HCI was returned to the Buckeye Trust. All is well. But some interesting points remain. For example, it is clear that the law firm of Buckingham, Doolittle & Burroughs is the legal representative for Buckeye Trust. But—and here's why Roadway got such instant cooperation where a news publication and a state legislator could not—they are also, according to the 1985 Standard and Poor's Register, the lawyers of Roadway Express, Inc. and Roadway Services, Inc. So this law firm was handling the affairs of both Buckeye and Roadway all along. Even if Roadway officials have no power over Buckeye donations—and it seems they don't—are we to believe that there was no *communication* about such a huge donation by a trust based on Roadway stock to officers of the Roadway corporations before this flap began? And if there was, why didn't Roadway officials complain about it themselves if they're so pro-gun? It may be finished, but the Buckeye/Roadway/HCI flap has left many unanswered questions of public interest. Finally, is this an unusual case, or does it represent just the tip of a much bigger iceberg of improper contributions by other trusts? We may never know.

A word of advice: If you try to *tell* this story to somebody, you'll find, as I have, that it's impossible. The story is so strange and contorted that you have to see it in print just to keep track of it. Try telling it and see for yourself. Take my advice, save yourself the trouble. Have your friends read this book instead.

THE FAT CAT CONNECTION

When it comes to foundations and their Gun Grabber shenanigans, one thing is sure, though: R. H. Durst of New York City's Durst Foundation gave $150 for Proposition 15. The George H. Gund Foundation of Cleveland heavily subsidized the "Handgun Control Staff" of the U.S. *Conference of Mayors*. The David R. Hirsh Foundation of Beverly Hills gave $1,300 to Proposition 15. The Moss Foundation gave $1,000. How much more Foundation money went to Gun Grabbers we simply don't know.

Well, back to more mundane Gun Grabber hijinx with Proposition 15: Clorox Co. of Oakland, makers of a well known household bleach and many other products, gave $2,000. Clorox employs 5,800 workers and made $913 million in 1984.

Collins Foods International, Inc. of Los Angeles, whose chairman and chief executive officer is James A. Collins, gave $1,000. The 8,850 employee-firm made $395 million in 1984.

Community Psychiatric Centers of California gave $1,000.

The direct mail consulting firm of Craver, Mathews, Smith & Co. of Arlington, Virginia, gave $5,000. This, too, is an interesting donation, but not so bizarre as the Buckeye Trust story. Craver, Mathews, Smith & Co. (CMS) is a prominent liberal direct mail firm which has handled left-of-center candidates and organizations such as the National Organization of Women, the National Abortion Rights Action League, the *American Civil Liberties Union*, and the Sierra Club Legal Defense Fund. CMS was fired as consultant for the Democratic National Committee when they aided the Draft Kennedy committee in 1980, but was rehired in 1981. They handled John Anderson's presidential campaign in 1980, Morris Udall's presidential campaign in 1976, and have also acted as consultants for Sen. George McGovern, Sen. John Culver, and Sen. Birch Bayh. Roger Craver—The "C" in CMS—sits on the editorial board of Campaigns and Elections magazine. Robert Smith—the "S" in CMS—like the other principals in his firm, worked in the Common Cause organization. Smith was also a former community organizer for New York City and other private youth groups. He has a B.A.

in political science and sociology from Berkeley.

The late Justin Dart, Sr., who was chairman of the executive committee of the board of directors of Dart & Kraft, gave $10,000. Dart & Kraft is famous for Kraft cheese and is a holding company manufacturing, marketing and distributing food products, packaging, plastics and chemicals. Their revenue is listed in Standard & Poor's Register as $9.7 billion. Neither their revenues nor the senior Dart's donation is peanuts.

Dearden's, a Los Angeles firm retailing furniture, appliances, TV and audio equipment and fine jewelry, gave $2,000 of its $16 million revenues to Proposition 15.

Golden State Mutual Life Insurance of Los Angeles gave $300.

Joseph M. Goldenberg, president of the $35-million-a-year Goldenberg Plywood & Lumber Co. of Los Angeles, gave $1,250.

Carter Hawley Hale Stores Inc. of Los Angeles gave $1,000. Philip M. Hawley is chairman of the board, chairman of the executive committee and chief executive officer of the $3.63 billion firm, which employs 54,000 people.

Armand Hammer, chairman and chief executive officer of Occidental Petroleum Corp. gave $50,000 to Proposition 15. Occidental has 41,000 employees and revenues of $19.7 billion. Bob Considine wrote a biography of this now quite elderly man, entitled The Remarkable Life of Dr. Armand Hammer. Hammer was born in the United States in 1898 and earned an M.D. at Columbia before building his father Julius' millions into billions. Instead of remarking on Dr. Hammer's huge donation to the Gun Grabbers, let me reprint without comment the written text of a telephone message that took place on May 11, 1922 from Moscow to Petrograd (modern Leningrad):

"Today I wrote a letter of reference to you and your deputy for the American Comrade *Armand Hammer*. His father is a millionaire and a Communist (he is in *prison* in America). He has taken out our first *concession*, which is very advantageous for us. He is going to Petrograd to be present at the discharge of the first wheat ship and to arrange for the receipt of machinery for his concession ((asbestos mines)).

It is my earnest request that you issue orders at once to see that there is no red tape and that reliable comrades should personally keep an eye on the progress and speed of all operations for this concession. This is of the utmost importance. Armand *Hammer* is travelling with the director of his company, *Mr. Mishell.*"

The call was placed to Grigory Evseievich Zinoviev, chairman of the Petrograd Soviet and of the Communist International, by Vladimir Ilich Lenin, first head of state of the Soviet Union. The text of this call may be found in English exactly as printed above in Volume 45, page 544, of V.I. Lenin, Collected Works, Progress Publishers, Moscow, second printing 1976. Earlier editions have different page numbers. The Russian language edition has different volume and page numbers. The italics in the text are from Lenin's original note in Russian.

Of course, this is all ancient history. Hammer has since served on several philanthropic and governmental committees in the United States and is known as a perceptive supporter and collector of art and as the benefactor of the Armand Hammer Foundation. Whatever his politics, he acts a lot like a capitalist.

To continue with donors to Proposition 15: Handgun Control, Inc. itself contributed $55,000 along with a loan of $136,000. HCI also acted as the intermediary for donations from Henry Van Amerigen, a retired American in Paris in the amount of $5,000; from Crawford Greenwalt, former DuPont board chairman, $1,000; and from Warren Zimmerman, a foreign service officer in the U.S. Embassy in Moscow, $500.

Hechinger Co. of Landover, Maryland, a retailer of lumber, building supplies and hardware with $309 million in revenues and 3,700 employees, gave $2,000. Mr. John W. Hechinger, the company's president, gave another $1,000.

Estee Lauder, Inc., the well-known New York cosmetics firm, gave $5,000.

The Los Angeles Dodgers gave $500 for Proposition 15.

MCA, the $1.59 billion entertainment giant headquartered in Universal City, California, gave $11,000.

Natomas Company of San Francisco, engaged in crude oil and natural gas exploration and production as well as petrol-

eum marketing, shipping and real estate, gave $5,000 of its
$1.66 billion revenues.

Pacific Mutual Life Insurance Company of Newport Beach,
California, gave $5,900.

David Packard of Hewlett-Packard fame gave $7,500.

Max Pavlevsky, ex-chairman of the board of Xerox Data
Systems gave $50,000 to start up Proposition 15.

Victor Palmieri, a Los Angeles attorney involved in the
Iranian hostage negotiations, lent $89,164 to Proposition 15.
Martha Palmieri gave $10,000.

Sol Price, a San Diego business executive, gave $11,500.

PWM Insurance Services of Los Angeles gave $5,000.

Steven C. Rockefeller, a New York City business executive, gave $10,000.

Stanley Sheinbaum, a University of California regent, gave
$8,100.

Southern California Edison Co. of Rosemead gave $5,000.

Henry Weintraub, president of Diener Hauser Bates Co.
Inc., the New York advertising agency—with 207 employees
and $30 million revenues—gave $50,000. That's as much as
Armand Hammer gave and Weintraub is nowhere near as
rich.

Wisley Foods, Inc., gave $5,000.

Whittaker Corp., the Los Angeles firm that manufactures
metals, chemical coating products, electronic and fluid control devices and biomedical materials, gave $1,000 of their
$1.6 billion sales.

Harold Willens, the Los Angeles millionaire running the
Proposition 12 campaign for a nuclear freeze gave $700.

TAKE MY MONEY.PLEASE: THE HANDGUN
CONTROL, INC. POLITICAL ACTION COMMITTEE

In order to understand HCI's Political Action Committee,
we need to dip into history for a moment. Wherever there is
political liberty, you will find "a division of the society into
different interests and parties," James Madison stated in The
Federalist Papers (Number 10—"Factions: Their Cause and
Control"). These factions, he went on, can create great mischief, but the cause of factionalism cannot be removed without bringing on a condition worse than the disease—the

destruction of liberty itself.It is only by having a great variety
of competing interests, Madison argued, that security is provided against any one interest being able to oppress the rest.
Madison, the father of the Second Amendment, here stated
the.pure essence of pluralism.

That also explains the virtue of Political Action Committees. These controversial committees have caused widespread handwringing because they're felt to give "special
interests" more political power than their numbers alone
would indicate. It would be easy to go along with this kind of
thinking, but it would be wrong.Worry about concentrating
American political power in a few hands might have been
justified in 1974 when there were only 608 PACs—and even
at that, those 608 were divided up into 89 corporate PACs,
201 for labor and 318 for trade, membership and health
groups.

Such worry about one-sidedness might have been quite
real back in 1948 when Maurice Rosenblatt founded one of
the first PACs, the National Committee for an Effective Congress (NCEC) with the support of such noteworthy liberals as
Eleanor Roosevelt. But ideological balance was provided in
1974 when conservative political strategist Paul Weyrich
founded the Committee for the Survival of a Free Congress
(CSFC) and in 1975 Roger Stone, Charles Black and Terry
Dolan formed the National Conservative Political Action
Committee (NCPAC). By 1985 there were 4,009 PACs, and
1,053 were not connected to any corporation, labor organization, trade group, membership group or health group. More
than half of these "non-connected" PACs were ideological in
nature, trying to help elect individuals who agreed with their
political philosophies, and PAC political philosophies spread
all over the map from left-wingers who have been praised in
Soviet publications to right-wingers who have been praised
by Jerry Falwell, and everything in between.

In other words, PACs have done exactly what James
Madison said was necessary to guard the liberty of the whole:
they've proliferated into such a great variety of competing
interests that security is provided against any one interest
being able to oppress the rest. And so what I have to say next
is not in any way a complaint against Political Action Commit-

tees themselves, but is merely an expose of Gun Grabber donations to HCI's PAC. I would not be upset if the Gun Grabbers turned the tables and published lists of pro-gun PAC supporters. It's all on the public record. Defenders of the Second Amendment have no reason to hide their support. People who want to vote the Second Amendment out of existence may have.

And so, for the edification of gun owners and the annoyance of Handgun Control Inc. Political Action Committee, here's what the public record says, as contained in HCI reports to the Federal Election Commission in Washington, D.C. I've limited the list to contributors of $500 or more. It would take a whole chapter to list all the smaller contributors. First, here's what high-dollar supporters gave to HCI-PAC for the 1982 elections:

Thos. Boal of Chicago Illinois,	1-4-82	. . . . -$500.00
Thomas A. Cohen of Mill Valley California,	1-12-82	. . . -$500.00
Richard J. Dennis Jr. of Chicago Illinois,	12-28-81	. . $2500.00
Thomas A. Dennis of Chicago Illinois,	12-28-81	. . $5000.00
Helen M. Garrison of Morgantown West Virginia,	12-28-81	. . . $500.00
Steven C. Rockefeller of Middlebury Vermont,	8-9-82	. . . . $1000.00
Mrs. John Sylvester of Washington D.C.,	1-18-82	. . . . $500.00

Now that's only $10,500, which I found a bit surprising, but quite a bit more than that came to HCI-PAC from smaller donors. We've already seen a good deal of where Gun Grabber money came from for Proposition 15, and there's no point belaboring the fact that some Fat Cats don't like guns. Now let's see what HCI-PAC did with their loot in the election season of 1981-'82. I'm going to do something to you that you may not like: print a long list. I'm doing it so you can see exactly when and to whom HCI-PAC gave election money and to give you some idea of the detail required in Federal Election Commission PAC reports. I won't do this to you again when I cover the 1984 election season late in this chapter, so don't worry about it. We'll do an overall analysis for that one.

HCI-PAC DONATIONS TO POLITICAL CANDIDATES,
1982 ELECTION:
Candidate - Party - State - District - Contribution Date -
Amount

Rep. Joseph Addabbo, D, NY-7	6-7-82	$500.00
Rep. Daniel K. Akaka, D, HI-2	6-7-82	$500.00
Rep. Ike Andrews, D, NC-4	6-7-82	$1000.00
Rep. Bill Archer, R, TX-7	10-4-82	$250.00
Rep. Michael D. Barnes, D, MD-9	6-7-82	$250.00
	10-4-82	$250.00
Rep. Jim Bates, D, CA-4	8-18-82	$500.00
Rep. Berkley W. Bedell, D, IA-6	8-5-82	$500.00
Rep. Howard Berman, D, CA-26	7-28-82	$500.00
Rep. David E. Bonoir, D, MI-12	6-7-82	$300.00
	9-8-82	$300.00
	6-22-81	$100.00
	1-27-82	$100.00
Rep. Bob Borski, D, PA-3	8-18-82	$500.00
	9-29-82	$500.00
Rep. Barbara Boxer, D, CA-6	8-5-82	$500.00
	10-4-82	$250.00
Robin Britt for Congress (NC)	10-4-82	$1000.00
Jerry Brown (ex-governor of California, unsuccessful challenger for U.S. Senate seat)	5/11/82	$250.00
	6-3-82	$1000.00
	10-15-82	$1000.00
Rep. Phil Burton, D, CA-6	6-7-82	$500.00
	9-8-82	$500.00
	10-4-82	$250.00
Sen. John Chafee, R, RI	6-3-82	$1000.00
Rep. Bill Clay, D, MO-1	5-19-82	$150.00
	6-22-81	$100.00
Rep. Cardiss Collins, D, IL-7	6-7-82	$250.00
	9-8-82	$300.00
Rep. John Conyers, D, MI-1	6-7-82	$500.00
Rep. Bill Coyne, D, PA-14	6-7-82	$250.00
Rep. George Crockett, D, MI-13	6-7-82	$500.00
Bill Curry for Congress (CT)	10-26-82	$500.00
	10-20-82	$500.00

Lloyd Cutler for Congress (IA) [former White House counselor]	
	8-18-82 . . . . $500.00
	10-18-82 . . $4500.00
Rep. Ron Dellums, D, CA-8	5/11/82 . . . . $250.00
Rep. Julian Dixon, D, CA-28	6-7-82 . . . . . $500.00
Rep. Brian Donnelly, D, MA-11	6-7-82 . . . . . $250.00
Rep. Tom Downey, D, NY-2	6-7-82 . . . . . $150.00
	8-5-82 . . . . . $500.00
	11-4-81 . . . . $100.00
Rep. Bernard Dwyer, D, NJ-15	6-7-82 . . . . . $400.00
	10-22-81 . . . $100.00
Rep. Bob Edgar, D, PA-7	5/5/82 . . . . . $250.00
	10-4-82 . . . . $750.00
	10-15-82 . . $1000.00
Rep. Don Edwards, D, CA-10	6-7-82 . . . . . $400.00
	10-4-82 . . . . $250.00
	9-23-81 . . . . $100.00
Erwin for Congress (CA)	9-8-82 . . . . . $125.00
Rep. Dante Fascell, D, FL-15	5-19-82 . . . . $250.00
	10-4-82 . . . . $250.00
Rep. Vic Fazio, D, CA-4	6-7-82 . . . . . $500.00
Rep. Edward Feighan, D, OH-19	5-26-82 . . . . $500.00
	8-5-82 . . . . . $500.00
Dick Fellman in '82 (NE)	10-26-82 . . . $500.00
Rep. Geraldine Ferraro, D, NY-9	5-19-82 . . . . $250.00
Rep. Thomas Foglietta, D, PA-1	4/27/82 . . . . $500.00
	9-8-82 . . . . . $500.00
Rep. Martin Frost, D, TX-24	8-18-82 . . . . $250.00
Rep. Robert Garcia, D, NY-21	6-7-82 . . . . . $250.00
Rep. Sam Gejdenson, D, CT-2	6-8-82 . . . . . $250.00
	10-4-82 . . . . $250.00
Rep. Bill Gray, D, PA-2	6-7-82 . . . . . $500.00
Rep. Bill Green, D, NY-18	5-26-82 . . . . $150.00
	1-27-82 . . . . $100.00
Rep. Frank Guarini, D, NJ-14	6-7-82 . . . . . $250.00
Rep. Tom Harkin, D, IA-5	5-19-82 . . . . $250.00
	8-20-82 . . . . $250.00
Herb Harris, D lost VA-8	7-14-82 . . . . $500.00
	10-4-82 . . . $2000.00
	10-15-82 . . $2500.00

Rep. Cecil Heftel, D, HI-1	5-19-82 . . . . $250.00
Hogan for Congress (CO)	10-4-82 . . . . $250.00
	10-15-82 . . . $250.00
Rep. Jim Howard, D, NJ-3	8-18-82 . . . . $500.00
	10-4-82 . . . . $500.00
Rep. Steny Hoyer, D, MD-5	10-4-82 . . . . $500.00
Kaptur for Congress (OH)	8-18-82 . . . . $500.00
	10-4-82 . . . . $500.00
Rep. Robert Kastenmeier, D, WI-2	6-7-82 . . . . . $500.00
Sen. Edward Kennedy, D, MA	4/21/82 . . . $1000.00
	5-19-82 . . . $1000.00
	8-18-82 . . . $1000.00
Kostar for Congress (KS)	8-18-82 . . . . $500.00
	10-4-82 . . . . $250.00
Sen. Frank Lautenberg, D, NJ	9-8-82 . . . . $1000.00
	10-4-82 . . . $1500.00
Rep. William Lehman, D, FL-13	6-7-82 . . . . . $150.00
	10-4-82 . . . . $250.00
	6-2-81 . . . . . $100.00
Rep. Mickey Leland, D, TX-18	6-7-82 . . . . . $250.00
	9-8-82 . . . . . $300.00
Rep. Sander Levin, D, MI-17	10-15-82 . . . $500.00
Rep. Mel Levine, D, CA-27	9-8-82 . . . . . $500.00
Rep. William Lipinski, D, IL-5	10-4-82 . . . . $500.00
Paul McCloskey, R, CA—lost Senate Republican primary	
	6-3-82 . . . . $1000.00
Rep. Stewart McKinney, R, CT-4	6-7-82 . . . . . $250.00
Rep. Ed Markey, D, MA-7	6-7-82 . . . . . $250.00
Martinez for Congress (CA)	9-8-82 . . . . . $500.00
	10-4-82 . . . . $500.00
	10-15-82 . . . $500.00
Americans for Masiokas (MI)	10-4-82 . . . . $125.00
Rep. Nick Mavroules, D, MA-5	8-20-82 . . . . $250.00
	10-4-82 . . . . $250.00
Maxwell for Congress (IN)	9-8-82 . . . . . $125.00
Rep. Romano Mazzoli, D, KY-3	5-19-82 . . . . $500.00
	9-8-82 . . . . . $750.00
Joe Merlino for Congress (NJ)	8-5-82 . . . . . $500.00
	6-28-82 . . . . $500.00
	10-4-82 . . . $1000.00

Sen. Howard Metzenbaum, D, OH	5/3/82 . . . . $1000.00
	8-20-82 . . . $1000.00
	10-4-82 . . . . $900.00
	9-23-81 . . . . $100.00
Rep. Barbara Mikulski, D, MD-3	8-5-82 . . . . . $500.00
Rep. George Miller, D, CA-7	5-25-82 . . . . $250.00
	10-4-82 . . . . $250.00
Rep. Joseph Minish, D, NJ-11	7-27-82 . . . . $250.00
Rep. Parren Mitchell, D, MD-7	6-7-82 . . . . . $250.00
Rep. Joe Moakley, D, MA-9	6-7-82 . . . . . $500.00
Toby Moffett, MA lost Senate race	5/3/82 . . . . $1000.00
	8-5-82 . . . . $1000.00
	8-18-82 . . . $2000.00
	10-4-82 . . . . $900.00
	11-19-81 . . . $100.00
Steve Monsma for Congress (MI)	10-29-82 . . $5000.00
Rep. Bruce Morrison, D, CT-3	10-4-82 . . . . $250.00
	10-15-82 . . . $750.00
Sen. Daniel Moynihan, D, NY	6-7-82 . . . . $1000.00
Offner for Congress (WI)	10-26-82 . . . $500.00
Rep. Thomas O'Neill, D, MA-8	6-7-82 . . . . $1000.00
Richard Orloski for Congress (PA)	8-18-82 . . . . $500.00
	10-4-82 . . . . $500.00
Rep. Richard Ottinger, D NY-24	6-7-82 . . . . . $250.00
	10-15-82 . . . $250.00
Rep. Jerry Patterson, D, CA-38	6-7-82 . . . . . $250.00
Rep. Donald Pease, D, OH-12	10-4-82 . . . . $500.00
Rep. Claude Pepper, D, FL-14	5/18/82 . . . . $500.00
	10-4-82 . . . . $250.00
Peter Peyser for Congress (NY)	8-5-82 . . . . . $500.00
	7-14-82 . . . . $500.00
	10-4-82 . . . $1000.00
Rep. John Porter, R, IL-10	6-7-82 . . . . . $500.00
Rep. Charles Rangel, D, NY-19	6-7-82 . . . . . $250.00
Rep. Peter Rodino, D, NJ-10	1-4-82 . . . . $1000.00
Rep. Robert Roe, D, NJ-8	7-27-82 . . . . $250.00
	10-4-82 . . . . $250.00
Rep. Benjamin Rosenthal, D, NY-8	6-7-82 . . . . . $150.00
	9-14-81 . . . . $100.00
Rep. Marge Roukema, D, NJ-5	10-4-82 . . . . $500.00

Rep. Ed Roybal, D, CA-25	6-7-82	$500.00
Rep. Marty Russo, D, IL-3	10-4-82	$250.00
	1-27-82	$100.00
Rep. Martin Sabo, D, MN-5	6-7-82	$500.00
Rep. James Scheuer, D, NY-11	6-7-82	$250.00
Rep. Claudine Schneider, R, RI-2	6-7-82	$50.00
	8-5-82	$250.00
	3-30-82	$100.00
	10-15-81	$100.00
Rep. Pat Schroeder, D CO-1	5-19-82	$500.00
Rep. Charles Schumer, D, NY-10	10-4-82	$250.00
Rep. John Seiberling, D, OH-14	5-19-82	$500.00
George Sheldon for Congress (FL)	9-3-82	$500.00
	10-4-82	$1000.00
	10-15-82	$1000.00
Rep. Larry Smith, D, FL-16	6-18-82	$500.00
	10-4-82	$250.00
Rep. Stephen Solarz, D, NY-13	6-7-82	$150.00
	9-23-81	$100.00
Sen. Spark Matsunaga, D, HI	6-7-82	$1000.00
Spratt for Congress (SC)	9-22-82	$500.00
Rep. Pete Stark, D, CA-9	6-7-82	$150.00
	8-18-82	$250.00
	10-4-82	$250.00
	6-10-81	$100.00
Rep. Louis Stokes, D, OH-21	6-3-82	$500.00
Rep. Gerry Studds, D, MA-12	6-7-82	$250.00
	10-4-82	$250.00
Tablack for Congress (OH)	10-15-82	$500.00
Rep. Robin Tallon, D, SC-6	10-26-82	$500.00
Rep. Tom Tauke, R, IA-2	10-4-82	$500.00
Rep. Robert Torricelli, D, NJ-9	6-18-82	$500.00
	8-5-82	$500.00
	8-18-82	$250.00
	9-8-82	$500.00
	9-23-82	$3250.00
Sen. Paul Tsongas, D, MA	5/11/82	$300.00
Rep. Bruce Vento, D, MN-4	8-18-82	$250.00
Mayor Harold Washington (Chicago)	6-7-82	$500.00

Rep. Henry Waxman, D, CA-24	6-7-82	$150.00
	9-8-82	$300.00
	10-4-82	$450.00
	6-22-81	$100.00
Rep. Ted Weiss, D, NY-20	6-7-82	$250.00
Rep. Alan Wheat, D, MO-5	9-27-82	$500.00
Rep. William Whitehurst, R, VA-2	7-27-82	$500.00
Rep. Howard Wolpe, D, MI-3	8-18-82	$500.00
	10-4-82	$250.00
Rep. Sidney Yates, D, IL-9	6-7-82	$500.00
Rep. Clement Zablocki, D, WI-4	10-4-82	$250.00
Robert Zimmerman (D, lost, NY-4)	6-18-82	$500.00

Now if that's not enough detail to make your eyes go funny, I don't know what is. I'm sure you recognize the names of many anti-gun-bill sponsors and co-sponsors on this list. But we ought to say something about other anti-gun advocates in politics who may or may not have received financing from Handgun Control Inc.

You remember John B. Anderson, don't you? He is a former congressman who also ran for president in 1980. He once said, "I favor a waiting period before a handgun can be purchased to allow a criminal records check; a strengthening of rules for commercial handgun dealers; the registration of all handguns at time of purchase or transfer; a license to own a handgun; a mandatory prison sentence for all persons using a handgun in a crime; and a ban on the sale of small, cheap, low-quality handguns."

Mayor Marion Barry of Washington, D.C. supports the District's "handgun freeze" ordinance.

Tom Bradley, former mayor of Los Angeles, supported Proposition 15 and probably lost his 1982 California gubernatorial campaign because of it. Ironically, a decade earlier he perhaps had a premonition of his own political defeat when the spoke at an anti-gun U.S. Conference of Mayors meeting: "The political climate indeed is warming up to the need for aggressive federal action to remove the handgun from our society. But I should note that elected representatives will probably be faced with the backlash of some one-issue voters who will go to the polls to vote against you. We need to be prepared for that." Did Bradley remember his own words the night he didn't become governor?

Speaking of governors, former California Governor George "Pat" Brown sat on the HCI National Committee.

Roland Burris, Illinois State Comptroller, sleeps with a handgun "right at the head of the bed," but he supports a nationwide ban on handguns.

Barbara Bush, wife of Vice-President George Bush, said in 1980: "I'll give you an instance where I differ with George. You know George has always been against gun control. For thirty-five years I've been for gun control."

Jane Byrne, while mayor of Chicago, participated in various anti-gun rallies.

Former President Jimmy Carter said in 1976, "I favor registration of handguns, a ban on the sale of cheap handguns, and reasonable licensing provisions including a waiting period."

Clark Clifford, former U.S. Secretary of Defense, supported Proposition 15.

New York Governor Mario Cuomo said in 1983, "I want to discourage the profligate use of weapons. The fewer the weapons the better."

The Democratic Party entered into its 1980 platform this statement: "The Democratic Party supports the enactment of federal legislation to strengthen the presently inadequate regulations of the manufacture, assembly, distribution and possession of handguns and to ban Saturday Night Specials."

Mayor Diane Feinstein of San Francisco gave $500 to Proposition 15 and supported her city's attempt to enact a handgun ban. She also sits on HCI's National Committee.

Vice-Presidential candidate Geraldine Ferraro co-sponsored HR 40 in 1981, which called for a ban on the ownership of all handguns, and in 1983 she co-sponsored HR 1543, which requires local gun shops to report the names of gun buyers directly to firearm manufacturers for easier tracing by the Gun Grabbers at the U.S. Bureau of Alcohol, Tobacco & Firearms.

Judge Hortense Gabel of New York City in late 1981 fined a New Jersey gun owner $2,500 to be paid to an anti-gun organization in order to avoid a prison sentence for inadvertently running afoul of New York's strict gun law. Some justice!

William Ruckelsh...us, twice director of the Environmental Protection Agency sits on the HCI National Committee and supported Proposition 15. In 1976 he teamed up with HCI Chairman Pete Shields and said, "The vast majority of people are calling out for handgun control and they need organization."

John Shay, Jr., president of Marygrove College in Detroit, following the shooting of Sister John Clement Hungerman in early 1984, called for stronger gun control laws while objecting to legislation enacting capital punishment.

Now, in the 1983-'84 election season, we had some more high-dollar contributors.

CONTRIBUTIONS OF $500 AND UP TO HCI-PAC FOR 1984 ELECTION
Henry F. Harris of Philadelphia 10-18-84 . . . . $5000.00
C.C. Herman of Washington, D.C. 10-12-83 . . . . $500.00
Ellen Bayard Kennelly of Greenville DE 10-29-84 . . $500.00
William Kovacs of Los Angeles CA 10-27-83. . . . . $500.00
Sarah B. Lefferts of Washington D.C. 10-17-84 . . . . $1000.00
Walter S. Rosenberry III
    of Englewood CO 10-6-83 . . . . $1000.00
Marjory Wynne Smith of Pacific Grove CA
    10-23-84 . . . . $1400.00

Now instead of giving you the itemized list of HCI-PAC recipients for 1983- 84, we'll do an overall analysis. HCI-PAC spent a total of $97,322 for the 1983-84 election campaign according to the 1984 Federal Election Commission Year End Report covering political activity through December 31, 1984. They contributed money to 113 Democrats and 13 Republicans. Democrats received 87.1 percent of HCI-PAC's contributions and Republicans received 12.9 percent. HCI-PAC backed 72 incumbent winners and one winning non-incumbent challenger; they backed 5 incumbent losers and one losing non-incumbent challenger. Their won- lost percentage was .935, which ranked them fifth in effectiveness behind Associated Milk Producers (.957), National Rifle Association (.953), National Right-to-Life Committee (.941) and National PAC (a pro-Israel PAC) (.938), according to a study by Larry Boyle in the Spring 1985 issue of Campaigns &

Elections. By comparison, the National Organization for Women ranked 19th out of 20 with a .548 percentage.

What does all this mean? It should be pretty obvious: the Gun Grabbers have cultivated a hard corps of Fat Cat donors and are cultivating friends in high places with the best of plows—money. This combination of finance and politics spells grave danger for the rights of gun owners. The only solace we can find in these facts and figures is that American politicians are for the most part honest and conscientious people—Gun Grabber campaign contributions and lobbying dollars may buy access, but they're not likely to buy specific performance. In other words, the Gun Grabbers can buy their way into a Congressman's door, but they can't buy votes.

6

The Non-Shooting Stars: Celebrity Gun Grabbers

WHENEVER A GUN OWNER ATTENDS A SUPERMAN movie, buys a product shown in a commercial sponsoring a Star Trek re-run, or buys a Kris Kristofferson record, he is funding those who seek to deprive him of his guns. Numerous actors who appear as anti-crime cop heroes in television programs are interested in disarming their viewers so they can't defend themselves against street-wise felons.

Remember Jack Lord, star of "Hawaii Five-O"? Once when asked about gun-control legislation, Lord said: "I think all guns should be taken out of the hands of citizens. It's a lot of bunk about sportsmen going out to shoot a little deer." When asked if he meant all guns, including rifles, should be taken away from individuals, he responded: "Yes, absolutely."

As *Chicago Daily News* columnist Norman Mark said of Lord's views: "Imagine that here is a man who stars in one of the most violent series on network television. He believes that senators who battle TV violence are 'headline-grabbing,' that 'life is violent,' and that 'you cannot do police format without violence.' Yet he opposes rifles and handguns in the homes of Americans. I wish I could understand how Lord does what he does (on Five-O) and believes what he believes (about guns)." Mark concluded: "The thought processes of TV stars can sometimes be mysterious indeed."

Television programs biased against gun owners can be broadcast without fear of any equal-time rebuttal. In one "Streets of San Francisco" segment, "Lt. Stone" (Carl Malden of American Express travelers checks fame) was showing a handgun owner a tour of a foundry where confiscated crime guns were being melted down and cast into manhole covers.

143

Stone was showing the gun owner what should be done to all handguns: when the camera zoomed in close and he made an impassioned plea that all viewers should ask their legislators to prohibit handguns to save lives and "stop a bullet."

Surprisingly, a number of anti-gun movie stars make their career by appearing in "shoot 'em ups." A trio of 1968 gun-control ads appeared in the *Washington Post, The New York Times*, and the *Los Angeles Times* which urged readers to "write or telegraph your Senators, Representatives, Presidential Candidate, State Legislature immediately! Ask them to join with those listed . . . in supporting strong gun legislation now."

Some of the more notable stars lending their names to this campaign included: Elizabeth Taylor (who financed the ads, costing about $18,000); Warren Beatty, the late Yul Brynner, Sammy Davis, Jr., Mia Farrow, James Garner, Dean Martin, Cliff Robertson, Robert Ryan and Rod Taylor. At the same time these ads appeared, these same actors appeared in the following gun-packed flicks: Warren Beatty in "Bonnie and Clyde," the late Yul Brynner in "Villa Rides," James Garner in "Hour of the Gun," Dean Martin in "Bandolero," Cliff Robertson in "The Devil's Brigade," and Robert Ryan in "Hour of the Gun."

Some celebrities are either really hypocritical or have learned from the error of their earlier anti-gun ways. In 1968, Sammy Davis, Jr. helped Elizabeth Taylor gather co-signers for a series of ads promoting the passage of "strong gun legislation now" legislation, which became the federal Gun Control Act of 1968. Sec. 922 (a)(1) of that act makes it unlawful for "any person" except a licensed dealer to "ship, transport . . . any firearm or ammunition in . . . foreign commerce."

Barely a year after Sammy Davis' advocacy for stronger federal gun-control laws, customs agents seized a revolver and ammunition from him when the American entertainer arrived at London Airport on June 28. Commenting upon his brief detention, Davis said: "I have a permit to carry a gun in America, but the customs informed me the laws are different in Britain and *quite rightly so.*"

A decade after entertainer Dean Martin co-sponsored the same 1968 ad as Sammy Davis, Jr., Dean was fined "$192 in a

Beverly Hills municipal court and placed on one year's probation for carrying a loaded concealed weapon." When Dean
had been stopped in May 1982 on suspicion of drunken driv-
ing, the police found a .38-caliber pistol concealed in his boot.

Although he had registered the gun as required by California law, he didn't have a carrying permit. Martin pleaded
no contest, and afterwards said: "I carried the gun for protection. But I was ignorant of the laws, new laws I guess. I'd like
to carry a gun, but I know I can't. The bad guys have all the
good luck."

Jane Fonda is another Hollywood Hypocrite when it con-
cerns firearms. You remember this upstanding patriotic
American heroine, the one pictured "manning" a communist
North Vietnamese anti-aircraft gun during the Vietnam War?
After her friend John Lennon was shot to death in December
1980, "Freedom Fighter" Fonda appeared at a memorial service to denounce American permissiveness toward handguns
and made a plea for more effective handgun control.

However, according to a Maryland journalist Robert
Taylor, she "herself may have made a material contribution to
that complaisance toward handguns with a highly lucrative
film that she had made almost four years earlier called 'Fun
With Dick and Jane,' since much of the fun referred to in the
title derived from robbing banks at gunpoint."

Taylor claims, "Although 'Fun' was released seven years
ago, its influence on suggestible people is still being felt. It is
still shown on campuses and videotapes can be purchased or
rented. The indulgent tolerance toward handgun crime that a
light-minded film of this kind engenders is utterly cruel in its
effects."

"Jane Fonda's flirtation with handguns certainly did not
alienate the news media," according to Taylor, who noted "of
nine reviews that appeared in the Film Review Digest Annual
for 1977, from all over the country, not one expressed any
distaste for the theme." Evidently, Jane Fonda loves handguns as long as they're making her piles of money.

Hollywood Handgun Homicide Humor is very widespread
among Tinsel Town directors and actors. When "Going in
Style" was released, its bank robbery scene was reviewed by
R. H. Gardner of the *Baltimore Sun* as, "A Gentle Comedy

About Old-Timers" and "one of the film's funniest sequences
. . . so hilarious" was the skit where actor Lee Strasberg leaps
forward, brandishing a revolver, in order to cow two bank
customers.

Following the debut of "The Grey Fox" in Baltimore last
October—which is a story of a man who spends ten years
robbing stage coaches and railroad passengers—movie re-
viewer George Udel wrote that it is a "narrative about clearly
defined people and their burning desires to live by their own
standards." In abhorrence of Udel's crime permissiveness
view, Robert Taylor commented, "Standards, one assumes,
that include terrorizing unarmed people."

Following is a list of celebrities who have either lent their
name as a co-sponsor of the National Coalition to Ban Handguns (NCBH) or the National Committee to Control Handguns—which is now known as Handgun Control, Inc.
(HCI)—or who have donated funds to these groups, their
anti-gun referendums, or have attended or sponsored an
anti-gun rally.

As we review the anti-gun activities of the following movie
and television non-"shooting stars", to save on space the following code words have been developed to avoid repetition:

"Prop. 15": Refers to Proposition 15, which, as you will
recall from previous chapters, was the ballot attempt by anti-
gun organizations to induce the residents of California to pass
an initiative in Nov. 1982 which would have created a "handgun freeze" law statewide. The voters rejected the initiative
by a margin of two-to-one. The notation "Prop. 15" in a
celebrity's biography indicates support of the anti-gun initiative and notes the amount of financial support contributed
towards the measure's passage.

"NCBH Week": The National Coalition to Ban Handguns
(NCBH) sponsored, during the week of October 25-31, 1981,
a coordinated nationwide campaign of media personalities
who were induced to lend their names to this NCBH project,
which urged city politicians to ask their residents to participate in the NCBH's "National End Handgun Violence Week"
campaign and to surrender their handguns to the police without compensation. Those personalities with "NCBH Week"
following their name lent their name to this anti-gun drive.

"Taylor Ad": Following the assassinations of Sen. Robert Kennedy and Rev. Martin Luther King, Jr., Elizabeth Taylor financed a series of anti-gun ads which appered in major metropolitan newspapers, and asked various media personalities to co-sponsor her ads.

Following is a list of actors, columnists, educators and other public celebrities who have supported some anti-gun activity:

Jack Albertson, actor in "The Poseidon Adventure" and "Chico and the Man," supported Prop. 15.

Steve Allen, famous television humorist, songwriter, and host of "The Steve Allen Show" and "I've Got A Secret," lent his name to "NCBH Week."

Arthur Ashe, now-retired tennis pro, supported Prop. 15.

Ed Asner, star of "The Lou Grant Show," "The Mary Tyler Moore Show," president of the liberal-oriented Screen Actors Guild (since 1981), donated $400 for Prop. 15 through the Asner Family Foundation and lent his name to "NCBH Week."

Patty Duke, popular child actress in the "Patty Duke Show" and "The Miracle Worker," lent her name to "NCBH Week." Once while I was waiting to appear on the "Seattle Today Show" of the local NBC affiliate, I met Patty Duke and her husband at the time, actor John Astin, in the holding room. We began to chat and a pleasant conversation quickly developed. Patty then asked me, "What will you be talking about on camera?" "Gun control," I replied. She and her husband instantly began to gush over me. "Gun control! How wonderful! We're all for it!" they enthused. I told them, "I'm against it. I'll be speaking in defense of the rights of gun owners." Dead silence. If you're ever invited to a Hollywood cocktail bash, this should give you a good idea how to be the life of the party.

John Badham, director of Rastar Film productions, donated $2,300 for Prop. 15.

Jack Barry, emcee for "Break the Bank" (1976), "The Joker's Wild" (1976 and 20 similar quiz shows, donated $100 for Prop. 15.

Warren Beatty, best remembered for his roles in "Bonnie and Clyde" and "Reds," lent his name to the "Taylor ads."

Mrs. Milton Berle, wife of comedian Milton Berle, donated $100 for Prop. 15.

Leonard Bernstein, renowned composer, lent his name to "NCBH Week" and donated $500 for Prop. 15.

Stephen Bishop, rock n' roll musician, donated $225 for Prop. 15.

Peter Bonerz, who played the dentist "Jerry Robinson" in "The Bob Newhart Show,": participated in "NCBH Week" and donated $500 for Prop. 15.

Ray Bradbury, science fiction author, lent his name to "NCBH Week."

Lloyd Bridges, aquaman in "Sea Hunt" and airport manager in "Airplane," lent his name to "NCBH Week."

Albert Broccoli, motion picture producer of the James Bond films "Goldfinger," "Moonraker," "For Your Eyes Only," etc. and "Chitty Chitty Bang Bang," donated $500 for Prop. 15.

Mel Brooks, who loved firing his guns in "Blazing Saddles" and who also directed "Young Frankenstein," supported Prop. 15.

Jackson Browne, rock n' roll musician, forked over $150 for Prop. 15.

The late Yul Brynner, who apparently had no qualms about using guns in "Villa Rides," "Westworld," and "The Magnificent Seven," cosponsored the "Taylor ads."

Carol Burnett, ever-popular comedienne starring in "The Carol Burnett Show," lent her name to "NCBH Week."

Ellen Burstyn, actress in "The Exorcist" and "The Last Picture Show," supported Prop. 15.

James Caan, who didn't mind packing firearms in "The Godfather" and "A Bridge Too Far," lent his name to "NCBH Week."

Robert Chartoff, producer of the smash-'em-up "Rocky" and "Rocky II," donated $100 for Prop. 15.

Carol Connors, actor, supported "NCBH Week."

Paul Conrad, lent his name to "NCBH Week."

Thomas Cook, screenwriter, gave $120 for Prop. 15.

Alice Cooper, rock musician, supported "NCBH Week."

B. Cooper, publisher for TV Fanfare Publishers, Inc., donated $150 for Prop. 15.

Sammy Davis, Jr., a popular entertainer and singer who portrayed a gun-crazy crook in "Robin and the Seven Hoods," in 1968 helped actress Elizabeth Taylor sponsor a gun-control ad in New York City. Her agent said that Davis was "instrumental" in soliciting endorsements for her ad. In 1969 he was briefly detained while attempting to carry a handgun into England.

Phil Donahue, television host of his own "The Phil Donahue Show," participated with his wife, Marlo Thomas, in an outdoor rally with Chicago Mayor Jayne Byrne to urge city residents to surrender their handguns to city police during "NCBH Week."

Michael Douglas, actor in the violence-prone "Streets of San Francisco," and the adventure film "Romancing the Stone" in which he totes a shotgun, donated $450 for Prop. 15.

Richard Dreyfuss, bespectacled actor in "Jaws," "Close Encounters of the Third Kind," and "The Goodbye Girl," lent his name to "NCBH Week."

William Elliott, composer, gave $200 for Prop. 15.

Mike Farrell, who played "Capt. B. J. Hunnicut" in "M*A*S*H," supported "NCBH Week."

Farrah Fawcett, lion-maned starlet who frequently shot handguns in "Charlie's Angels," lent her name to "NCBH Week."

Robert Foxworth, actor in "Falcon Crest," attended a public-relations event to publicly support Prop. 15.

Art Garfunkel, actor and still a singer after splitting with Paul Simon of "Simon and Garfunkel," gave $100 to Prop. 15.

Lou Gossett, Jr., actor in "Roots," "Backstairs at the White House," and "An Officer and a Gentleman," donated $100 for the passage of Prop. 15.

Elliot Gould lent his name in promoting a fund-raiser dinner for the NCBH in Washington, D. C. in June 1982. Asked why he had come all the way from L.A. for the event—and why he appeared in his NCBH T-shirt—Gould said, "I'm actively involved in disarming the world." He also supported "NCBH Week." Gould is remembered for starring roles in "M*A*S*H" and "Bob & Carol & Ted & Alice."

Joel Gray, fast stepping dancer in "Cabaret" gave $150 to Prop. 15 and supported "NCBH Week."

149

Valerie Harper, who won an "Outstanding Lead Actress in a Comedy Series" award in 1975 for her show "Rhoda" and who was a co-star in "The Mary Tyler Moore Show," attended a 1978 "Handgun Control, Inc. & National Coalition to Control Handguns" fund-raiser dinner.

Mariette Hartley, most famous for appearances in Polaroid commercials with James Garner, donated $300 to Prop. 15.

Goldie Hawn, blond actress in "Laugh-In," "Private Benjamin," "Cactus Flower" (which won her a best-actress Oscar), "Shampoo," and "Protocol" lent her name to "NCBH Week."

Buck Henry, author of "Heaven Can Wait," spent $150 in support of Prop. 15 and lent his name to "NCBH Week."

Hal Holbrook, actor in "Midway," "All the President's Men" and "The Senator" was once listed as being on Handgun Control, Inc.'s National Committee.

Graham and Jo Anna Jarvis—Graham was actor "Charlie Haggers" in "Mary Hartman, Mary Hartman," donated $1,075 to Prop. 15.

Norman Jewison, director of the short-lived "The Judy Garland Show," blew $2,975 for Prop. 15.

Shirley Jones, motherly actress in "The Partridge Family," lent her name to "NCBH Week."

John Kearney, a sculptor in Chicago, designed a statue portraying handguns being formed into plowshares.

Chaka Khan, a rock group, lent its name to "NCBH Week."

Jack Klugman, who played the medical examiner in "Quincy," attended a 1978 "Handgun Control & National Coalition to Control Handguns" fund-raising dinner.

William Kovaks, a Hollywood director, gave $150 for Prop. 15.

Kris Kristofferson, popular actor, singer and songwriter, supported "NCBH Week."

Peter Lawford, late Kennedy in-law and well-known actor who played in "Paris After Dark," "The Longest Day" and portrayed a gun-toting crook in "Ocean's Eleven," served on Handgun Control Inc.'s National Committee.

Norman Lear, television producer and writer for "All in the Family," "Maude," "Mary Hartman, Mary Hartman" and "The Baxters," and president of the American Civil Liberties Foundation of Southern California, not only gave $2,200 for

Prop. 15 but also lent his name to "NCBH Week."

Hal Linden star of the cop sit-com "The Barney Miller Show," gave $100 for Prop. 15.

Kenny Loggins, rock musician, cosponsored "NCBH Week."

Harry Logan, television producer with the Hewlett-Packard Co., gave $200 to Prop. 15.

Jack Lord, star of "Hawaii 5-0," said: "I think all guns should be taken out of the hands of citizens. It's a lot of bunk about sportsmen going out to shoot a little deer. Big deal." He was asked if he meant all guns, even rifles, should be taken away. "Yes, absolutely," he answered.

Dean Martin, of "The Dean Martin Show" and "The Dean Martin Celebrity Roast" and gun-toting actor in "Rio Bravo" and "Bandolero," lent his name to the 1968 "Taylor ads."

Steve Martin, comedian, a frequent guest on "NBC's Saturday Night Live" and actor in "The Jerk" and "A Wild and Crazy Guy," lent his name to "NCBH Week."

Marsha Mason, wife of anti-gun playwright Neil Simon and actress in "The Goodbye Girl," gave $500 for Prop. 15 and served on Handgun Control Inc.'s National Committee.

Marilyn McCoo, singer and emcee of "Solid Gold," lent her name to "NCBH Week."

Margaret Mead, late anthropologist, once served on the advisory councils of Handgun Control, Inc. and National Coalition to Control Handguns.

Dr. Karl Menninger served on Handgun Control, Inc.'s National Committee.

Graham Nash, singer and composer with "Crosby, Stills and Nash" (1969), lent his name to "NCBH Week."

Laraine Newman, comedienne starring in "Saturday Night Live" and "Hot Wax," lent her name to "NCBH Week."

Randy Newman, comedian, gave $150 for Prop. 15.

Shirley Knight, actress, supported NCBH's "Survival Days" program in 1977 with DISARM.

Harry Nilsson, singer and songwriter of "Nilsson Schmillson" and "Midnight Cowboy" actively promotes the NCBH.

Leonard Nimoy, "Mr. Spock" in "Star Trek," gave $600 for Prop. 15.

Gregory Peck, star of "MacArthur," "Twelve O'Clock

High," "Moby Dick," "Snows of Kilimanjaro" and "To Kill a Mockingbird," gave $300 for Prop. 15.

The Police, a rock band, supported "NCBH Week."

Otto Preminger, renowned director, served on the NCBH's National Advisory Council.

Christopher Reeve, star of the recent "Superman" movies, lent his name to "NCBH Week."

Carl Reiner, director of "Oh, God" and "The Jerk," lent his name to "NCBH Week."

Nelson Riddle, composer of scores for "The Great Gatsby" and "The Untouchables," supported Prop. 15.

Cliff Robertson, actor in "The Devil's Brigade" who received a "Best Actor" Academy Award for "Charly" (1968), lent his name to the "Taylor ads."

Will Rogers, Jr., stage actor, serves on Handgun Control, Inc.'s National Committee.

Judith Rossner, author of *August* and *Looking for Mr. Goodbar*, in late 1983 joined the NCBH-PAC's Board of Review and commented "I'll do anything to help stop the current handgun lunacy."

Robert Ryan, gun-toting actor in "Hour of the Gun" and "Anzio," lent his name to the 1968 "Taylor ads."

Telly Savalas, lollypop-sucking star of the long-running and violent police show "Kojak," once opined: "I don't like guns! I've always been against them and I don't give a damn how much my private attitude against guns goes against the Kojak image. I don't like people having guns at all!"

Susan Saint James, actress in "MacMillan and Wife," gave $350 for Prop. 15.

George Segal, actor in "Who Is Killing All the Great Chefs of Europe?" and "The Owl and the Pussycat," lent his name to "NCBH Week."

Sha Na Na, a pop music band, lent its name to "NCBH Week."

Neil Simon, playwright of "The Odd Couple," "The Goodbye Girl," "Barefoot in the Park" and husband of anti-gunner Marsha Mason, serves on Handgun Control Inc.'s National Committee.

Frank Sinatra, ever-popular crooner, gave $250 for Prop. 15. through the anti-gun Californians Against Street Crime and Concealed Weapons campaign. Sinatra's contribution is laughable because of his heavy personal bodyguard.

Tom Smothers, of "The Smothers Brothers Show," lent his name to "NCBH Week."

Rod Stewart, pop-rock musician, donated $150 to Prop. 15.

Terry Southern, singer, lent his name to "NCBH Week."

Jean Stapleton, the actress who played Archie Bunker's wife Edith in "All in the Family," lent her name to "NCBH Week."

Rod Steiger, actor starring in "The Amityville Horror," "In the Heat of the Night" and "Lion of the Desert," served on advisory councils for Handgun Control, Inc. and the National Coalition to Control Handguns, and supported Prop. 15.

Loretta Swit, "Maj. 'Hot Lips' Houlihan" of the television show "M*A*S*H," donated $150 for Prop. 15.

Elizabeth Taylor, star of "Cleopatra," "National Velvet" and "Who's Afraid of Virginia Woolf," in 1968 sponsored an anti-gun ad campaign in several major metropolitan newspapers.

Rod Taylor, actor in "Dark of the Sun," lent his name to the "Taylor ads."

Marlo Thomas, of "That Girl" and wife of anti-gunner Phil Donahue, appeared with her husband in a public rally in Chicago supporting "NCBH Week."

Theodore Thomas, filmmaker, donated $135 for Prop. 15.

Gary Trudeau, creator of the "Doonesbury" comic strip, designed a poster to commemorate NCBH's "National End Handgun Violence Week" in 1981.

Dick Van Patten, actor in "Eight is Enough," lent his name to "NCBH Week."

Robert Vaughn, actor appearing in "The Man From U.N.C.L.E.," "The Towering Inferno" and "The Bridge at Remagen," lent his name in support of "NCBH Week."

Eli Wallach, actor who appeared in "Lord Jim" and "The Good, the Bad and the Ugly," served on advisory councils for Handgun Control, Inc. and the National Coalition to Control Handguns.

Dennis Weaver, gun-toting actor in "McCloud," "Gunsmoke" and "Stone," lent his name to "NCBH Week."

James Whitmore, star of "Will Rogers, U.S.A." and "Give 'Em Hell, Harry," serves on Handgun Control, Inc.'s National Committee and narrated HCI's "The American Handgun War" film.

Gene Wilder, actor, director and writer for such shows as "Blazing Saddles," "Silver Streak," "Stir Crazy" and "Young Frankenstein," lent his name to "NCBH Week" and donated $200 for Prop. 15.

Andy Williams, singer and entertainer,lent his name to "NCBH Week" and serves on Handgun Control, Inc.'s National Committee.

Robin Williams, comedian star of "Mork & Mindy," "Popeye" and "The World According to Garp," lent his name to "NCBH Week" and donated $300 to Prop. 15.

Henry Winkler, "The Fonz" in "Happy Days," donated $250 for Prop. 15.

Herman Wouk, author of "The Winds of War" and "The Caine Mutiny," donated $100 in support of Prop. 15.

There's more to the story of Gun Grabber Celebrities than their money contributions and endorsements of events. How good-sized segments of the whole entertainment treats the gun issue gives us something to think about, too. For example, consider how pro-gun movies are treated. When MGM-United Artists' anti-Soviet movie *Red Dawn* came out in 1984, it played to packed houses, stood at the top of the motion picture box-office charts for at least two weeks, and ranked high in the most-rented videotape charts for at least a year. The public liked seeing how easy it was for an invading Soviet army unit to disarm civilian Americans by simply reading gun registration lists—except for a few intrepid patriots who escaped to the wilderness to gather strength and find a way of fighting back.

But Gun Grabbing film critics hated *Red Dawn* with a passion. Admittedly, it was not an art film and had no pretensions to Oscar night kudos—it was straightforward entertainment, a well-constructed, well-acted, rip-roaring adventure story that happened to have a pro-gun message. Its success at the box office drove the critics nuts.

The National Coalition on Television blasted *Red Dawn* as the most violent movie ever made. Perhaps Coalition watchdogs don't know how to count, but *Red Dawn* had far fewer dead bodies than the *Star Wars* trilogy (Darth Vader's "Death Star" blew up a whole *planet*, remember?). Then, too, almost any World War II film epic, from *A Bridge Too Far* to *The Guns of August,* had a much higher body count. And any of the *Friday the 13th* blood-n-guts operas was graphically gorier by far. Not to mention Shakespeare's *Hamlet*—by the last scene everybody's dead but Horatio and Fortinbras. The major difference is that *Red Dawn* was clearly anti-Soviet. Could it be the TV Coalition has different biases?

The average American Gun Grabber couldn't handle *Red Dawn* either. A Michigan movie-goer wrote this to his local newspaper: "The film supports everything that is base and foolish about the current administration's attitude toward American/Soviet relations. It is not only an insult to the Soviet Union, it is an insult to the American public. The portrayal of the Russians as child-murdering, mindless machines, the obvious support of the NRA's ludicrous paranoia of gun registration—all would be comic, if they weren't dangerous tools to build the senseless wall that already exists between the United States and the Soviet Union."

No doubt this critic has been to the USSR to see how wonderfully free to own weapons its citizens are, has visited Afghanistan and marvelled at how thoughtfully the Russians murder Afghan children, and has walked the concrete wall around the Eastern bloc countries built by Soviet troops to keep out all us paranoid capitalists just aching to get into the workers' paradise. And by all means, let's not insult the dainty Soviet Union. They'd *never* want the U.S. to register guns, would they?

The Gun Owners of America honored John Milius, director of *Red Dawn,* for "dramatically depicting the importance in our time of the Second Amendment." At GOA's 1984 annual awards banquet in Crystal City, Virginia, media director Ed Nelson said, "Since he was panned by the critics, we thought that he deserved some special recognition for *Red Dawn,* which has several positive pro-gun messages in it."

The entertainment world must have a sense of the macabre, because even the most tragic celebrity event can be turned to use by the Gun Grabber cause. Such was the case in

155

the ironic 1984 twist of fate by which Jon-Erik Hexum, co-star of a CBS TV series with Jennifer O'Neill, the actress who wounded herself in the stomach in 1983 while handling a pistol, shot himself in the head with a blank-loaded Hollywood prop gun and died of the wound.

Hexum's death was ruled accidental by Los Angeles County coroner's officials. On Oct. 12, 1984, Hexum had just finished the final day's filming of the seventh episode of his TV series "Cover-Up" when he picked up a .44-caliber Magnum prop gun on the set and pointed it at his right temple. Hexum squeezed the trigger and fired the weapon. The concussion and paper wadding broke loose a piece of Hexum's skull the size of a quarter and drove it through the actor's brain. Massive hemorrhaging put Hexum into a deep coma because only a small portion of his brain was still functioning.

Hexum was rushed to Beverly Hills Medical Center where doctors performed five hours of neurosurgery. Hospital physicians said the actor's brain died Oct. 12. Authorities declared Hexum legally dead on Oct. 18. Hexum's mother Gretha agreed to the donation of the actor's heart, kidneys and corneas to organ banks.

Mike Gibbons, a prop handler for five television series, said he warns actors they can be harmed by the blanks in prop guns. Gibbons added, "If a man picks up a firearm and loads it and points it to his head, you're not going to be able to stop that." Gibbons said that stronger licensing laws would not affect the use of firearms on television and movie sets.

Hexum's mother Gretha and his brother Gunnar asked that people who mourn Jon- Erik's death send donations to Handgun Control, Inc. of Washington, D.C. The Hexum family would not comment on whether they supported gun control before the accident.

On that oddly bizarre note we end our harrowing journey through the world of the Gun Grabber. Gun owners should now have a sadly clearer picture of just what they're up against in maintaining their right to keep and bear arms. We've seen who the gun grabbers are, how they operate and where they get their money. If that doesn't worry you, nothing will.

Can something be done about it? Of course. Make sure all your friends read this book just as you have. And keep up your support for the organizations that work effectively to insure your right to keep and bear arms. Whatever you do, don't lose heart. Right makes might. We know we're right. In time we will prevail. We'll write a happy ending to this story yet.

But for now, as they say at the end of production in Hollywood, "That's a wrap!"

Index

159